Art and confrontation

France and the arts
in an age of change

STUDIO VISTA LONDON

Translated from the French by Nigel Foxell

Copyright © 1968 by La Connaissance s.a., Bruxelles

Published in London, 1970 by Studio Vista Limited, Blue Star House, Highgate Hill, London N. 19.

Printed in Belgium.

SBN 289 79758.6 (Paperback)
SBN 289 79759.4 (Hardbound)

Art and confrontation

Contents

Jean Cassou

Art and confrontation

There are periods in human history when the critical faculty grows more active and virulent, so that it appears predominant. More than that, it seems to absorb or sum up the other faculties, to become the very spirit of man. We are now witnessing one of these periods. It is not that man has arrived at an arbitrary, capricious decision to express himself at this time in a way that is essentially and integrally critical; it is rather that the material upon which man works, namely the world, has taken the form of a producer-consumer society.

Various sociologists, the most penetrating of whom is generally recognized to be Herbert Marcuse, have studied and described this change. It is a change that has made the world into an enclosed world; nothing exists outside it; it is, in the most exact meaning of the word, totalitarian. Its ends are to be found within itself. It produces in order to consume what it produces. The activities of the human spirit inside this enclosed world will in every case be purely technical; they will tend exclusively to ensure, develop, and perfect production and to administer the consumption of the objects produced. But the human spirit is volatile by nature and cannot be confined to these strictly practical needs; it aspires to free itself from such flat, monotonous constraint so as to take up a position outside the world, a position from which the world can be judged. It is therefore by an act of violence that the human spirit will perform one of its proper functions, that one which suddenly emerges as the main function, namely criticism. It is not a matter of examining the way such and such a wheel turns inside the totalitarian machine and effecting some improvements of an equally technical and practical kind. It is the machine as a whole that the human spirit considers. And the violence with which it tears itself away from the machine in order to judge it will have an impact on its judgment. This judgment too will be total and absolute. It will be a confrontation of the entire machine, a condemnation of its existence.

Thanks to an illegal breakout, this world can at present be examined from the outside, and what emerges is a producer-consumer society; in this context, the human spirit is aroused all the more to the violence of confrontation by the fact that it can find no place for itself here, unless it is prepared to see itself reduced to a routine supervisory function. If, in this world, it could expose conflicts like those in the economic, social, and mental order which its analyses brought to light in the capitalist world of the nineteenth century, then it would still have a chance and a hope of performing a role, a constructive role, in accordance with its proven procedure – that is to say by applying itself to dialectic. But the class that constituted one of the two poles in the chief conflict of the nineteenth century has become integrated into today's society; more and more it passively consents to take part in the game of production and consumption, and for the sake of a mess of pottage (refrigerator, car, motor bike, TV) renounces its mission as the agent of eventual subversion, that is to say to an act of the spirit. This, at any rate, is where it is being led by the political apparatus of its leaders, an apparatus which has become social-democratic and bureaucratic; in other words it is a docile element within the new society. This society has closed in on itself, on its own constant workings, and no longer fears that there may arise within itself or from itself the least cause for change. Convinced of its enduringness, it calmly trusts in its own technocratic whirr and hum.

The human spirit further declares that the things which fall within its province, the things through which it manifests itself by nature and necessity, are degraded by the system: they become nothing more than objects that are produced with a view to consumption, on a par with all the other objects enumerated in the system's catalogue of manufacture and sale. They are "cultural goods."

A culture seen in terms of "cultural goods" is not an easily definable concept. At the very least what we understand about it is that it intends to be conceived in terms of "goods," taking the form of possessions, property, patrimony, heritage, in accordance with the values of the stock exchange and the marketplace. If a culture conceived in these terms becomes the concern of a government department, it is inevitable that the head of the department constantly feel moved to admire the fact that we, the men of today, are charged with the memory of all the most disparate styles of the past. But this does not impose on us the responsibility for a style of our own. The only obligation this "culture" imposes

8

on us is to preserve the testimonies of the past, and perhaps even more to preserve the opportunity they provide for self-glorification.

In submitting to this rhetorical obligation, we forget that research into the past could, in certain ages, constitute a revolutionary effort and that, for example in France, the founding of the department of historic monuments was due to the innovatory impulse of Romanticism. If the men of that time were struck by the idea of *conserving* medieval churches, it was because these same men had *discovered* them. This discovery was part of a glorious, all-embracing revolution of sensibility and taste.

Inevitably, however, the producer-consumer society is incapable of lending the least vital feeling to the attachment due to the works of the past. The reason is that this kind of society is unable to recognize any evidence of life in these works. All it can see in them is things that have been made, established, completed. Consequently, it is itself unable to *make*. The regime by which this society is at present represented in France could never have dreamed of any of those great collective artistic enterprises that mark a regime and classify it forever as a *civilization*. The chimera called "culture" is sterile and sterilizing, quite the opposite of that living, concrete reality that is a civilization. Thus the present regime, in the name of "culture," scrapes monuments, lengthens them at the base, and takes care not to build any. No monument or monumental complex will be chalked up to its credit, and we in France are wasting our time to look for the daring necessary to conceive or attempt any kind of Brasilia. And yet there are vast spaces presenting it with such opportunities, for example Les Halles; there are voids to be filled, but it remains paralyzed before them. To be sure it took the initiative in paving certain streets in the Latin Quarter: in the roster of the great achievements of Parisian town-planning, this is nothing. At least the fear of the barricades under a similar regime inspired the wide boulevards that Haussmann cut through the capital. Finally, startling proof of this incapacity to build has been provided by the college at Nanterre. The French university had suffered from a shortage of space for a number of years, so that at last construction became necessary. The decision was made to build in the most horrible way possible, according to a wretched architectural plan; the site was sinister and desolate, in a slum area without any natural or social environment, and every precaution was taken to ensure that life could never emerge and develop in that place.

It is worth noticing that these were exactly the same precautions certain other regimes took when setting up their concentration camps. It was a matter of creating factories that operated with no end in view – they went through their own motions, and that was that.   Anything that might awaken the idea of a purpose – any action springing from the nature or spirit of man – was excluded from the site, the setting, and the buildings.   It would be a mistake to offer the retort that this operation nonetheless produced results and that one is justified in thinking it had an exterior aim, a finality, namely death.   I repeat, there was nothing about its operation to suggest that there was any concerted, methodical plan, a program leading to a result which, if we judged by appearances, might have seemed to be death.   Let us suspend our dumbfounded amazement, or whatever other sentiment it inspires in us, and examine the concentration camp as it actually was: it wasn't set up *for* death. If death became implicated in it, it became so in a subsidiary and adventitious way, not expressly, for if death had been the aim there would have been no need for such a colossal organization, such a formidable apparatus, such a deployment of staff and administration.   It is an abuse of logic to call these camps "extermination camps."   If extermination had been planned and decided on, as there appears to have been secret talk of doing at the time the Nazi camps came into being, it could have been brought about by swifter and less complicated means.   If there were preliminary discussions and an intention was formulated, we must realize that this was deflected from its goal to become reabsorbed in absolute technicality.   Reason, let us remember, operates by starting at one point and proceeding to another; in the case of practical reason, to an end; but the kind of reason to which the founders of the Nazi camps may have initially had recourse became excluded from the modus operandi of camps thus begun.   Anyhow the gates to these don't tell you that you enter them to die, but to work.   Work for what? You incorrigible logician, do you still want a goal?   The inscription at Auschwitz answers you, *"Arbeit macht frei."*   This is as much as to say that the work performed inside remains inside, producing nothing except the feelings that must be experienced by those who are condemned to do it – one is to feel free, which is nonsense. Unless this unreal feeling is the form under which the unreal product of this work is consumed.   Which is madness.   But didn't we say that reason had been excluded? When all is said and done, it is only the extreme, ideal aspect of any society that sees virtue only in the efficiency of its functioning. Thus the founders of the Nanterre campus deliberately swept aside anything that might distract from its functioning, a tree, a café; they had no aim in mind that could give the students access to a possible destiny; they have clearly shown what it means to create a pointless architecture and set an aimless mechanism in motion.   Whatever it may have been about this artificial piece of nothingness that set off the French student revolt, the symbolic character of the action is clear for all to see.

In its hostility to life, its inconsistency with every kind of initiative, in the stubbornness with which it exists only in an abstract permanence, the producer-consumer society emerges as the triumphant culmination of all bourgeois societies of previous ages, as the bourgeoisie *par excellence*. It is the perfect achievement of bourgeois philosophy. Such an achievement is rendered possible since there is no longer any revolution to fear, since the very idea of revolution is abolished. Revolution is an idea that could only come from the outside, and the outside is inconceivable; all that is conceivable is the immanence of the perpetual circuit of production and consumption. Order is definitely achieved in all fields, including that of the spirit. The productions of the spirit, of human genius, the works of thinkers and artists are considered as objects and treated as objects. Hence they only exist to be consumed by society along with all the other objects that it objectively consumes. They have only been made with a view to this consumption, without any questioning of their origin and destination. The whole comfort of bourgeois philosophy derives from this certainty, the certainty of ignorance. Society is oblivious, inevitably oblivious of the essential nature of these works, of knowing their quality of *creation*. These are creations. Herein lies their specific character, their specific difference. To confuse them with the goods which one possesses, which one exchanges according to price lists and quotas and enjoys like any ordinary goods is to degrade their specific differences to the level of the differences that fashion and publicity fabricate between two gadgets.

A remarkable example of the offhand manner which the technical consumer society adopts in relation to works of art is provided by the adaptations and digests of famous novels and the distortion they are subjected to by cinema, radio, and television. There is no need to dwell on the first of these industries, which publishes abridgments of such masterpieces as *War and Peace* and *Manon Lescaut*. *Manon Lescaut* is, in fact, much too long, and as the hours at our disposal decrease, their value increases. Even so, the practice is idiotic, particularly as its perpetrators rationalize their actions by pointing to the necessity of reaching children; hence the outrageous travesties of Victor Hugo or Jules Verne, *Don Quixote* or *Robinson Crusoe*. Here we encounter a combination of stupidity and greed which is best passed over in silence. If one mentioned them at all, it would be to express astonishment that their makers are not liable to the same penalties as forgers of banknotes; should our society indeed be reminded that it puts a price tag on works of art? But let us move on to the other industries,

11

the adaptations of novels for cinema, radio, and television. These are unique to our age, with its technical media of mass communication.

It is the glory of our century that it has invented various instruments that extend the creative power of the human hand and that have produced new arts with a character of their own; one in particular, the cinema, has developed in an extraordinary way and produced innumerable masterpieces that are among the greatest and most beautiful of all time. The role of this art form, as well as that of radio and television, in giving new life to the drama is unquestionably of supreme importance. Plays were written to be seen and heard; what a wonderful enrichment of eye and ear through screen and radio! The fact is that cinema, radio, and television are arts, like the theater, like music; it is right and natural that they should render mutual assistance, and when they do so, the one does not alter the nature of the others but on the contrary reinforces it, just as their cooperation reinforces and multiplies the pleasure that each gives us. But a novel transposed into cinema or television has lost its nature as a novel. It is something else. Doubtless an adapter with a *creative* gift can effect this transformation of a contemporary novel, and do it with the approbation and even the collaboration of a still-living author. In this case there will be creation stemming from creation. And it frequently happens that this second creation also will be original, vital, and moving – a masterpiece. But when we come to the novels of the past which have become part of our universal heritage, we experience a strange uneasiness: the characters, the settings, the episodes, the tone and tempo of the dialogue, the sentences, the style have a life of their own and are integrated into the collective consciousness of humanity, so that when such novels pass through machines invented by the present age they emerge with an ambiguous look about them, which is at once allusive and scarcely recognizable. This uneasiness is something that we feel to be peculiar to our own age. What has happened is that the inventions of the twentieth century, so admirable and wonderfully suited to creative use, have been perverted into channels that are opposed to creativity. They have been utilized in culture consumption. I will not pause over the fact that certain film, radio, and television adaptations of famous novels have had undeniable good qualities. If this is the case, so much the better. Or so much the worse, for it is the act of adaptation itself that we are questioning, and its qualities are secondary; we don't recognize them to be of the same order as the qualities of an entirely created work, a creation. And what we are discussing is indeed creation! We are discussing culture, a certain trafficking with the creations of the past, and when the machines of our industrial age take a hand

12

in it, this trafficking can reach amazing proportions. This trafficking spreads across the world wherever machines allow it and claims that it is thereby disseminating "culture," that is to say knowledge of the past, knowledge of the past's greatest novels, knowledge of art and genius, which spread, illustrate, and exalt the "spiritual values." These values are unassailable, they are hallowed, they can inspire trust, they are a number of excessively celebrated books that no one reads anymore, no one has any need to read them, which is the best proof of confidence that a book can be accorded; but everyone, everyone throughout the world has heard of them because of the publicity they have gained from these adaptations, and everyone knows them in this adapted form, in this phony version. And that is what is meant by the consumption of cultural goods.

Also consumer goods, easily consumed, are these visual works of art. Museums, exhibitions, international competitions, reproductions, reviews, series of art books, tourism, and of course radio and television again, as well as dealers, collectors, enthusiasts, and critics reveal this accumulated knowledge of previous styles, which, as we have seen, officially define the meaning of the term "culture." This knowledge is the first step in the consumption of works of painting and sculpture, which our society organizes in the same way as it organizes the consumption of every other object. To this must be added the various forms of acquisition and enjoyment of these objects, whether they circulate on the market as opportunities for speculation or find a resting-place in a private or public collection. In any case, one element in these "objects" is and remains utterly neglected, namely their *subjective* side. Haven't we said that they were no more than objects? Objects set in the framework of an exclusively objective world where nothing is conceivable except objects? Now, these objects, whether we realize it or not, whether there exists any extrinsic subject capable of realizing it or not, are the creation of a certain individual with his own particular condition and destiny, with the result that he may deserve to be regarded as a person. The art of this artist-creator is an act of consciousness. It could be seen as such. Or it could be seen as a revolution, as historians see it – they study the history of these artists and place their art in history. As far as the artists of our own day are concerned, future historians will have to distinguish those in whom this same revolutionary quality may be discerned. But it is characteristic of bourgeois mentality, with its desire to maintain the status quo, to take no interest in history. That is why our society is content to group all modern artists within the indistinct, neutral mass of "producers," and not only the conformists, but also those whose works reveal some surprising traits. For the public, these traits will be nothing more than the unexpected, spicy little note that a shrewd producer gives to his products. But in this comprehensive reality consisting of the consumption of old or new works of art by a society whose existence proclaims itself, satisfies itself, and limits itself by consumption, Van Gogh or some equivalent artist of our own day cannot be considered on his own account – that is, in terms of what has been accomplished by the one and is potential in the other. Let us confine ourselves to the case of Van Gogh because the evidence cries out more clearly and significantly where the assembled facts are at our disposal. The case of the man who was Van Gogh. Van Gogh is no more. But it isn't enough to state that he is no more. What must be said is that he *is not*. Van Gogh is not Van Gogh now. Society has sterilized him in its laboratory, he has been vulgarized as part of its encyclopedic material, he has been retailed in samples in its salesrooms, splendid houses, and official buildings. Some might be tempted to confuse this abstracting operation with scientific concern and pious memory. It is in fact nothing of the sort, for scientific concern and pious memory restore things to their living reality. But it is just that living reality that bourgeois philosophy is intent on destroying. What it claims to deny, or, to be more precise – for there is no conscious intention or effort involved – what is ignores, what fails to exist for it, is creation, and that there was, in Van Gogh, by Van Gogh, creation. The moral imperative of the bourgeois is to see to it that nothing happens, and his article of faith is that nothing ever has happened. "No histories!" the worthy bourgeois exclaims. And today when with the producer-consumer society he is convinced he has arrived at the peak of his desires, he can say, "No history!" This society is founded upon the estrangement from history, the decline and fall of history. It is known that history existed, since there are historians, but that existence is a spectral one, *as if nothing had happened.* And it is necessary that nothing should have happened because the assertion is that nothing will happen in the future.

What a strange thing it is that "culture" should be the name we must give to this consumption! It can only be compared to the digestion of a boa. These works of art – to better determine our thoughts let us consider them by taking the example of Van Gogh: there they are, bled white, enervated, emasculated: What relation, we ask, can exist any more between them and us? What is this familiarity, so blunted, mute, cold, indifferent, coarse, mechanical, somnambulistic, with which we pick up and pass from hand to hand these empty, limp objects that were once *creatures*? Creatures, children of creation, unique forms, as alive as flames, molded with passion and grief, the fruit of a capacity to feel and express so excessive that they attain a very convulsion of madness... One feels stupefied as by some absurd enigma when one tries to measure this disproportion between the event which was the creation of the works of Van Gogh by their creator, and the way in which they are utilized and manipulated by what a consumer society calls "culture."

The creation of the works of Van Gogh is indeed an event. And I must repeat that these works, like all works of art, have their place in history, are historic realities. To have a place in history is to have a place in time, which implies movement and change. Change is brought about by criticism of what is, and by bringing into being what is not. In every work of art, in the oeuvre of every artist, and in the entire artistic output of an age, two mutually related aspects must be recognized in the creative act: an opposition to some point or other in the existing artistic situation, and an invention of ideas and new forms. This is how art manifests itself as art. If it is reduced to continual reiteration, it is no longer art but the decay of art, an academicism. Herein lies the mortal danger to art. On the other hand, our society, like others, deems that to live is to perpetuate its present identity, not to change but to remain as it is. Thus they are assured of a solid base to their institutions, of adherence to the rules of succession, of the effectiveness of their police, and of the scant likelihood that history, i.e. revolution, can disturb this order. This program seems to have been carried out more scrupulously and rigorously by bourgeois society than any other. Our present society is still a bourgeois society, even though, in order to establish itself, it has had to deal with conditions unknown to the society that immediately preceded it, namely the bourgeois capitalist society; the latter, in the same measure as it developed, saw the rise of its antithesis, the proletariat. Here we are at present in a more advanced period of the industrial age, and we have already pointed out that our society, the producer-consumer society, tends to integrate the proletariat in the same way as it tends to integrate all possible contradictions. This is what makes it so essentially bourgeois, or rather this enables it to realize the supreme ideal of the bourgeoisie, the elimination of any risk of change. It will consequently be in a position to immerse itself in an absolutely perfect mechanization, which is essential to absolute immobility and similar to the regular circulation of the stars within the celestial spheres of ancient cosmogonies. This ideal, by its extreme nature monstrous and deathlike, enables us by contrast to feel to the full what is meant by the consciousness of man in a historical and creative society.

It is surely with a feeling of freedom and joy that we shall approach, in order to study, that critical activity that by necessity belongs to the artistic process. This process cannot come about without a break with the taste, feelings, and state of mind of the moment (which is indeed a *state*), without resolutely destroying certain things that *are*, finally making them into things that *have been*. It is well known how the school of Gauguin complained about impressionism: "mindless... limited... it contains no thought...," etc. True, these complaints were not based on any objective criterion, but on the plain fact that Gauguin and his friends were what they were, and hence different from their predecessors. As for the impressionists, they had never dreamed of exalting the values of the intellect, but those of the senses; their vocation had not been to give form to intellect but to paint impressions. These artists too had been what they were, and their art, in the course of history, could not overstep the limit of their being. Impressionism lasted one generation – that of the impressionists. This isn't a truism – it's an ontological truth. But this affirmation of being must be accompanied by aggressiveness and polemics in order to become completely established, in order to satisfy our desire that every living man should have a sense of his responsibility, if there is to be a quickening of our appetite for human sympathy, fullness, and solidarity. This assertion must, in *addition*, be negation. The impressionists lived to see their work rejected by their successors Gauguin, Cézanne, who were masters of intellectualistic construction; but the impressionists had themselves rejected the manner of painting of their day, that care, which they considered ridiculous, for providing such an exact imitation of things as to make them appear solid. The tendency of the impressionists, on the contrary, was to view things as ephemeral and convey a feeling of their mutability. Out of this they created an esthetic system, but this system, like systems of government, could not claim to be enduring; it could only claim to uphold the art they practiced, which inevitably disappeared with them since it was a manifestation of their being.

It would, of course, be a mistake to infer that the schools and styles, as well as the great creative figures (or geniuses, to use a much maligned but necessary word), who have contributed in the most significant way to the establishment of these schools and styles must be juxtaposed in history like separate, isolated phenomena, each in its pigeonhole. Impressionism, cubism, and all the revolutions of modern art exist by virtue of those who have produced them, and their survival can only mean mechanical repetition, inertia, academicism, and death. It is no less true that revolutions have influences and effects which appear in time, act upon time, so that these revolutions are not only events that have taken place, but continuing sources of life.   They will give rise to new creations in unforeseeable combinations which will perhaps contradict their very origins, but which will reveal aspects of them that were previously unsuspected.   There is a wealth of currents and counter-currents, mutual influences, repercussions and surprises that in the course of time makes the fine tissue of the life of the spirit, which is completely distinct from the sequence of cause and effect in physical reality, the domain of law, necessity, and the sciences.   The elements to be discovered in the life of the spirit and particularly in the world of art cannot be simply defined by means of observation, experiment, logic, calculation, and other rational methods and thereafter be dismissed.   The intelligence that discloses the elements of the life of art cannot exhaust them, because they in turn take on the generative quality of the reality that gave rise to them; they too become renewal, transformation, creation.   In the world of creation, the created is itself creation, everything is creation.

But we must not forget that this creation which so multiplies and proliferates itself is effectual in proportion to the critical virulence it brings to bear – a virulence that is expressed not only in terms of resolutions and theories but that is revealed in the production of works whose sole existence, presence, and quality are themselves an accusation, a questioning, a confrontation of contemporary art, its styles, themes, and the concept of the world it is dependent upon, and finally of the society that was founded upon this conception of the world. Thus the negative side of all art is a necessary concomitant of its positive side, an organic condition of its existence.   It plays the part by resisting.   This opposition is not always as clear-cut as those we have just given as examples, which occurred in modern times when the idea of revolution has enjoyed increasing favor to the point of becoming virtue, and esthetic revolutions have succeeded one another at an ever-increasing pace.   Other periods in history have unfolded more slowly, and so transformations in art have been slower then too. It would be pointless for us to retrace here the details and ramifications of the frequently debated problem of the relationship between the evolution of the arts and the evolution of contemporary society, to which they are so closely linked that they are said to be the expression of it.   Nevertheless, we must mention how in the culminating circumstances in which this society in transformed into another of an extremely different kind, the arts are less an expression than an anticipation.   And so they are spoken of as "avant-garde" – at least this is a term still favored only recently.   A valid, vital artist removes himself from the society he contests, he repudiates its conventions and practices his art as he understands

17

it. By his innovations, his research into new methods, his original combinations of formal elements, and by his affinity with such little-prized aspects of exterior reality and social life, he appears to give form to subsequent modes of feeling. He seems to anticipate the style that will suit the next generation, which will find him immediately intelligible. We should not be surprised by such a favorable reception of works that, at the time of their creation, had seemed so difficult. We find ourselves wondering whether we are confronted with the miracle of a people who suddenly understand the language of a foreigner, or the miracle of a foreigner who suddenly speaks the language of the people he will travel among next year. This is perhaps what actually happens. The artist we have judged to be valid and vital is this stranger. He feels a stranger to his world; he presumes that his inventions, which are shocking to it, stand a chance of according with the thoughts and feelings of the world of the future, even though he doesn't know how, nor is it his business to know. And he himself has the sensation of being in the future. It has been said often enough that there is something of the prophet in the poet; but a prophetic frame of mind is in fact inseparable from the consciousness of the poet who veers away from his own age and therefore awaits another and at the same time realizes that the world too is change.

What we find are more or less simultaneous transformations in every field of human activity, whether technical, economic, ideological, political, mental, or moral, and these undergo mutual adjustment whereby they tend to converge. This is how a new system is contructed, or, to use a less precise term, a new style of life. When this world of the future is formed, it will be free from old prejudices, and old conventions will be a dead letter to it. Then it can understand the work of our artist who is ahead of his time. In this context the word "understand," which is so irritating in the vulgar remarks that cheapen it, must be allowed a meaning that is appopriate to art. To understand a work of art is to be conscious that it truly is a creation, that it contains a reaction against the official norms of the moment and an aspiration toward *something else*. This is the kind of reaction and aspiration with which the historian is continually concerned; they are to to found in every field, especially politics, bringing about the disappearance of a worn-out world and the coming of a new one. It naturally goes without saying that no literal parallel can apply in every respect, for we must always allow for the contingencies of actual life.

No matter what form it takes and even if we allow for the more or less delicate nuances whereby we become aware of a transformation in the arts, this transformation is always critical. The arts, insofar as they are creative, are an

18

argument against the procedures generally adopted at the time, expressing themselves by choice of subject, figure, and motif, by new forms or, to be more exact, the new manner of producing forms, their disposition in space and the variations in the very representations of space, by new techniques and by the dominance given to line, color, volume, rhythm, to such and such a material or natural agent like light and atmosphere or to such and such a mental faculty, the evidence of the senses or the desire for structure and geometry. In the long run the arts destroy the system that the existing society has delayed in turning to account in the images that were created in accordance with its own procedures and principles.

Gods, princes, governments, myths, customs, and codes put their mark upon the art of an age and establish its conventions. The need arises to thwart these conventions. And the manifestation of this need is art. Established religion imposes and regulates the forms of art, but art little by little, or sometimes by a sudden effort, undertakes to represent something other than the ideas, beliefs, symbols, and scenes of the prevailing religion, as if this freedom had never been prohibited, or as if it had to gain the right to shatter the prohibitions and finally not to care about them any longer. Thus, objects of no liturgical significance are seen to appear in the Virgin Mary's room, articles of mere domestic use, while in the background, which is the end of the room and not an abstract background, can be seen a window opening onto a familiar landscape or a city with its buildings and activities. The mood that determines these changes may seem peaceful and touching, but such changes are nonetheless acts of a critical mentality, discarding or questioning a certain order. Moreover a realistic movement in art is always revolutionary, and by its tendency to depict the tools, attributes, costumes, and behavior of ordinary people it often offends the prejudices of the artistic public of the age, who favor the exclusive and aristocratic subjects to which propriety demands that art should be limited. But by offending these prejudices, art frees itself from rules and limitations and thus regains its true nature, which is – to use another discredited and dangerous word – liberty. But we cannot do without this word if we are to give full meaning to the terms of criticism and confrontation. We shall then understand that liberty is not an *a priori* characteristic of art, but art itself manifesting itself in practice and in deed.

Thus, realism has appeared at various critical and revolutionary points in history. In the Middle Ages it was a force for secularization and laicization, giving rise to a consideration of earthly values. At other times it has burst the bloated bubble of mythologies, allegories, history paintings, and pompous or state portraits in which a regime, whether monarchical or bourgeois, projected what it thought – and wanted others to think – of its deeds and splendors, its contentment and unshakable stability. Courbet was not a revolutionary merely because, as a citizen and as a friend of citizen Proudhon, he professed wild republican opinions and because he was involved in the Commune and the removal of the column in the Place Vendôme, but just as much because he was an artist and an artist of genius who, with the aid of certain historical circumstances, made a manifesto and a challenge out of "realism." In the circumstantial clothing of realism, artistic creation was for him essentially and categorically polemics, revolution. But idealism too can be polemics and revolution; history provides many examples (we have seen that Gauguin is a case in point) of an art that is governed by the intellect and its methods and that with an extreme authoritarianism imposes its reasons and maxims and the peculiarity of style and manner that flow from them; thus it broke the superstitious concern that the academies of the time nurtured for reality. Only this "reality," or what they referred to as such, had nothing in common with that of the realists, with nature, with life. It was a shriveled, outworn reality, which had fallen into the same degraded state as the society that advocated it.

No matter what direction we move in when exploring the history of forms, we find moments when artistic invention – more or less prematurely and with varying degrees of consciousness – comes to terms with the subversions and discoveries of the collective conscience. At the time of the revolution that was renaissance humanism and the epic conquest of the universe whereby it manifested itself, we find once again the activity of the critical spirit of man in the artistic revolutions that anticipated it, accompanied it, and commented upon it – the replacement of two-dimensional representation by depth, a delight in perspective, numbers, etc. All this exuberance in the figurative arts implies an extraordinary intensity of pleasure in discarding former figurations where man was depicted as subordinate to his beliefs, hierarchies and subsequently abolished constraints. But this abolition is firmly established in our consciousness only because there was a discarding of forms. This abolition made itself *evident*. It appeared in the world of visible things.

Thus a critical, negativist will is inherent in the creative process. Therein lies a certainty that must be recognized and borne in mind if we are going to grasp all the vigor and positive significance of that process. This is the condition under which artistic inventions carry the day. The dawn can only hope to produce what is of the color of dawn if it is born of a struggle with hours which, though beautiful in themselves, are of the color of night.   Here we find confirmation of that simple truth that beauty is not a transcendental idea but an energy.

To know the beauty of a picture or a poem is to know the energy which is concentrated within it, and which is so alive only by virtue of the force of contradiction that originally spurred it.   When this energy occurs in art, it is known by the special name of imagination.   Doubtless this term may seem to refer only to the positive, purely affirmative side of the creative process.   It means the capacity to form images, to engender visual, poetic or musical creations which are added to those of nature, of our ordinary existence, and of our industry.   They are additions to the world, to its resonance, scent, and splendor.   They are said to express its meaning, but this equivalence does scant justice to all that is so unfathomably strange and moving in the act of imagination.

However, the formation of images doesn't come about of its own accord like a natural function; it is not an automatic production governed by necessity, or a capricious, gratuitous act.   It has its being in time, space, life, conditions, and circumstances, and consequently in confrontation.   And nothing is imagined, however gracious, enchanting, and brimming with happiness it may be, without – by the very fact that it has been imagined – implying some discord.

It is this discord that makes it live.   Let us not deceive ourselves about the integrity of the imaginative faculty by seeing in it a need for compensation. It exists no more as the need of compensation for weaknesses, misfortunes, and defeats than as aimless reverie or vain, irrational mind-wandering.   It aspires with all its might to create something that has not hitherto existed, and it is both natural and vitally necessary that this aspiration should in part derive from the rejection of things that are, the indefinite prolongation of whose existence could only produce fatigue, disgust, and anger.   Some of this anger will therefore be found in the thing which does not yet exist and is to be made, this thing that the imagination imagines and into which it puts all its care, having recourse to all the powers whose assemblage, arrangement, and economy constitute *ars*, its means and its manner.

In commenting on Delacroix, Baudelaire spoke of imagination as the queen of faculties.   We can thus understand that in the moment of *crisis* out of which an artist's creation springs, imagination is the essential motivating force.   It is what gives an artist in the process of creation the feeling, perhaps objectively unjustified but vital and necessary, that he is transported on a limitless upsurge, that nothing he undertakes *will be beyond his capability*; this is quite different, and how much greater, truer, stronger, communicating a much more vital sense of pride and, let us say it, liberty than if he were to do (or give himself the illusion of doing) what he wanted to do (or what he gave himself the illusion of wanting to do).

Similarly, in the moment of crisis out of which springs not the individual creation of an artist but the collective creation which we call a revolutionary movement, it is again imagination which is the driving force. A confrontation with the existing society arises, but those who do the confronting are aware that their confrontation is only valid if it is accompanied by a creative upsurge – hence the appeal to the imagination. Thus one of the inscriptions which the inspiration of the moment spread over the walls of the colleges and the streets of Paris during May and June 1968: *Imagination takes power*. The significance of this declaration is both concentrated and dynamic; thus it is applicable to every event of a revolutionary nature, whether it occurs in the progression of societies or in that of the creations of the mind, or else in the one total progression which is the history of man. History stands still when the critical spirit, dissatisfaction, the desire for change for one reason or another abandons the game; and suddenly there is no more game, nothing plays, nothing thinks, nothing happens; if there is activity it is a mechanical activity that leads nowhere. But imagination arises and intervenes. It takes power and is itself power.

Michel Ragon

The artist and society

Rejection or integration

In May 1968, many artists adopted an attitude of rejection toward the repressive structure of the consumer society, or, if you prefer, of industrial civilization. There was refusal to collaborate with the existing power structure, a desire to shatter the framework of the art market; even art itself as properly understood was called into question.

The artist cannot escape from what is at once the fascination and the anguish of our age – an age whose civilization can only be roughly sketched, comprising as it does automatisms, regulations, and tyrannies – a civilization of automation and of programmed leisure. What a marvelous adventure it would be for the artist if he could integrate himself with the new city and become a technician in collective beauty, escaping from the easel picture and mantelpiece sculpture, no longer creating art for one, but for all! But suppose there should be a trap? By integrating with the city don't we become hostages? Even accomplices? Isn't the artist's role that of perpetual confrontation, a living example of permanent revolution?

Doesn't this attitude of rejection threaten to place us outside our time, confining us to a stance that is, when all is said and done, outmoded? In saying no to the evolution of society toward an apparently inescapable technocracy, aren't we going to stagnate in some ridiculous, outdated corner? Gandhi, as we know, came out against the machine, whereas Mao transformed the peasants into metal-workers, improvising "pocket forges" in every village. The consequence is that no one starves anymore in China, which is now self-supporting. As for India, it is reduced to begging from the great powers, and famine continues undiminished there.

Many artists may be tempted to move into the woods like Thoreau, to reject

23

the society of the machine like Henry Miller and Lanza del Vasto, to drop out. Who doesn't dream of his Polynesia? In the eighteenth century, when the world of the machine began to emerge, when the life of man in society began to be regulated, when the worker appeared, artists dreamed of the "noble savage."

But what if everyone were to adopt this attitude of retreat, and society became paralyzed? It would be a good opportunity to destroy the consumer society. But in order to replace it by famine? There has been no famine in Europe since the mechanization of agriculture. Multiply the number of "drop-outs" and clothes made of handwoven cloth will be worn and the wolf will be at the door again. And so will the soldiers of those nations that haven't chosen retreat.

The objection that could be leveled against contemporary artists before the "events of May" was precisely this attitude of retreat. They seemed to feel no concern for the evolution of the world, for the evolution of techniques, of architecture and town-planning. Isolated from a world which was in the midst of transformation, withdrawn into the island retreats of their studios, they produced superbly apocryphal works for the enjoyment of a few specialists. Their productions bypassed consumer society to the extent that they were not collectively consumed. The artist was like a master cabinetmaker to a few oil and steel kings. He produced exclusively for private collections and museums, thus putting himself outside the channels of popular consumption. The objection may be raised that the museums are part of these channels. But this isn't so. The art in museums is not consumed. It is placed outside our time. It is something one visits. It doesn't belong to the active environment of the city. It is an art of the past. Even a picture that was painted yesterday becomes, by the mere fact of being hung in a museum, as alien to daily life as a Sumerian work of art. It has retreated from life and passed into the realm of the timeless.

That artists should work exclusively for multi-millionaires and museums has struck us as so scandalous that we have pushed all possible forms of the democratization of art – multiple works, works that utilize industrial techniques and hence become industrializable, works integrated with contemporary architecture, sculpture-architecture, etc.

But however praiseworthy the idea of the multiple may be, we soon see that this process represents the kind of good intention that redounds to the profit of the capitalist consumer society. To multiply the number of petty art collectors is to reinforce the cult of private property in its most abominable form. It's the same as transforming proletarians into petty capitalists by means of home-ownership and the accumulation of gadgets and appliances through long-term credit. Seen in this context, the multiple becomes just another gadget. All that remains is to sell works of art on credit, or to rent them out so as to stimulate the appetite for buying, a ploy that has not been overlooked by certain galleries in search of a new market. The multi-millionaires constitute a very small clientele and one which is getting smaller, partly because they are a dying species and partly because they exist mostly in the Americas, and America is tending to snub a Europe by which it has itself been snubbed; hence the art market has fallen back on the elite among the proletariat – supervisory personnel. The multiple, which in most cases is a false multiple since it is made is a limited edition, as with prints, is principally directed at these supervisors. But editions can be enlarged so that the price goes down until the multiple comes within the budget of the skilled worker, and even of the unskilled laborer. One may reach the point of making multiples for garden apartments (the housing developments for supervisors) and others for Low Rent Housing Developments. One might even go so far as to sell multiples from catalogs in department stores and drugstores. This would be a form of democratization of art, just as home-ownership is a form of democratization of property. But all this would lead to quite the opposite of the socialization of art which seems to us the desirable end. One can imagine the result of multiplying easel pictures so that every citizen could hang one in his dining-room; a taste for collecting would arise among the masses. The spirit of the unique work, the speculative work, would nevertheless remain, and bargain sales of multiples would inevitably take place. Speculation would clearly be on a smaller scale than in the case of unique, unreproducible works, but it would be like dividing National Lottery tickets into tenths. More people would be able to play at collecting, that's all.

The multiple is the democratization of art as against the socialization of art. It is reform as against revolution.

So it is also with works that utilize industrial techniques and which therefore are industrializable. A certain amount of experience in this field has shown us that there can be something of an approach to the socialization of art in that the works are perishable, or so gigantic as to defy private acquisition. But in this alliance between art and industry it is generally art that suffers. Next to an engineer, the artist often looks like a handyman. The artist's primary forms are very often less remarkable than the primary forms of industry itself.

"What folly that painting should attract attention by its resemblance to things we don't admire at all in the original," said Pascal.

Yes, but it must be said in favor of the artists that certain of their works enable us to "see" properly those originals that we doubtless would not have admired if our attention hadn't been drawn to them.   When the Arc de Triomphe was wrapped in green cloth so that the workmen underneath could proceed with their resurfacing, they had achieved, without knowing it, Christo's masterpiece. But would we have admired this wrapping if Christo hadn't enabled us to see the beauty of wrappings?   The same with César's compressed cars or Arman's piles of bits of Renault cars.   None of these artist does better than the original, but they have "revealed" to us the beauty of the original.   In the same way, since Cézanne we no longer look with the same eyes at Mont Sainte-Victoire, although even he did not do better than the original.

It remains nonetheless that this "enabling to see" ultimately appears rather ridiculous.   Rudyard Kipling's disillusioned statement comes to mind:

"The vast majority of people are content to remain in studios and in a day that is not a day, to concoct studies that go by the name of 'color specimens,' which are achieved by means of pots and cans, rags and bricks.   Their worthless collection ultimately costs as much as a first class ticket to those new worlds where 'proportions' are given by sunlight."

As for works that are integrated with contemporary architecture, these are generally easel pictures that have been blown up to the dimensions of the wall, which the architect has willingly agreed to leave to the artist because he doesn't know what to do with it; often it's an architectural blunder that the mural painting is called upon to camouflage.   The artist is thus engaged as a tattooist, and it was with the thought of this aberration that Adolf Loos declared, "ornament is a crime."

If bad architecture needs ornament, great architecture can very well dispense with it.   A building by Mies van der Rohe, Le Corbusier, Candela, or Saarinen is itself a work of art.   Nothing is gained by adding a painting or a sculpture. Saarinen's TWA Terminal at New York is both an architectural marvel and one of the finest sculptures of our age.   The terrace roof of Corbusier's Unité d'Habitation in Marseilles, with its ventilating shafts, is a wonderful sculptural complex, and his chapel at Ronchamp is at the same time architecture, sculpture, and painting.

Insofar as architecture is a great autonomous creation, the artist is of no help to the architect or engineer.   There is no need of a painter or sculptor for the Verrazano Bridge in New York, the Palazzo di Lavoro at Turin, the parliament building in Brasilia, or the Secretariat at Chandigarh.   It's rather the mediocre architect who calls in the artist to help him.   Scant consolation.

26

The same applies to this form of integration of the arts as to the multiple. To place a sculpture on the lawn of a housing project or paint a mural in the lobby of an apartment building is a form of democratization of art, a form moreover for which there is ancient precedent, but this is a far cry from the socialization of art, for this would consist in offering the entire housing project an esthetic experience. Did I say housing project? Rather the entire society. And this could only be brought about by giving the visual arts a new meaning, by deliberately forgetting the picture and the statue for the sake of a veritable environment, an environment that would extend from man's clothing to his housing, from his objects of everyday use to his town-planning.

This has been grasped by those artists who have spent the last years proposing "environments" and creating happenings.

Unfortunately, for want of public acceptance, their "environments" remained "drawing-board environments," if one may put it that way. They didn't transform the framework of everyday life. Similarly there were happenings in Paris right up to May 1968, when the happening broke upon the capital.

For nearly two months the Sorbonne, the Odéon, and the entire Latin Quarter were permanent happenings. At the same time the city was rediscovering one of its functions, which is to create festivities. The Latin Quarter rediscovered another good feature of a city – the forum. It was only with the battles between police and students that it took on the aspect of a happening and of a holiday. As if to add to this impression, the police force wore costumes. They no longer looked like the ordinary police of joyless towns, but were transformed into a stage army with all the classic accessories of the theater – shields and knights' helmets. Common or garden policemen were transformed into gladiators. Thus they stood out even more from the students, who chose the most casual dress: blue jeans and shirts or sweaters, with sneakers and motorcycle helmets. The police were specially recruited from mining districts and poor agricultural areas, and their trappings made them the very image of proletarian despair. Unemployed young men were transformed into the C.R.S. (Compagnie Républicaine de Securité), landless peasants were transformed into a militia; the State had dressed them in black caparisoned with steel. They played their dismal role like the witches in Macbeth. They emerged from the depths of the ages, the depths of the country, the uttermost depths of despair and boredom. And the State hurled this refuse of the rural and urban proletariat, these outcasts of consumer society, against what is also a product of consumer society, its finest ornament, the student.

It is undoubtedly no coincidence that the man who introduced happenings to France, Jean-Jacques Lebel, and who now calls himself an "ex-painter," was the protagonist at the "capture of the Odéon." The "capture of the Odéon" was Jean-Jacques Lebel's great answer to the American happenings which he had been accused of weakly imitating. In one evening he did something better, bigger, and greater. He created a veritable "event."

This rediscovery of urban play is an important aspect of the May Revolution. Another was the reconquest of the Latin Quarter by its natural occupants, who had been driven into the student housing area at Nanterre[1] just as in 1871 the Paris Commune had been the reconquest of the city by the workers who had been driven by Haussmann and the speculators into housing parcelled out for them on the outskirts.

The May Revolution rediscovered the sacred feeling for festivities, for games of love and death, for outspread banners and posters papering the city walls. The Cuban Revolution too had previously rediscovered the sacred feeling for festivities, the collective life, the urban environment, and the socialization of art with giant posters and giant paintings. The painters of Cuba are permanently on exhibition along the walls of Havana. There the museum is the city. Nor is the city a museum-city. This is the true diffusion of art—an art to bathe in, to live with.

How, after the tremendous happenings of May and June in Paris, after the permanent happening of the Living Theatre in Avignon, which so scandalized the local inhabitants that the mayor lost his seat as a deputy in the legislative elections, how, after these happenings that have emerged from the laboratory to engulf the Festivities, can anyone still dare put on an indoor happening? How, after seventy cars were burned in the Latin Quarter and their carcasses long remained "on exhibition" in the unpaved streets, will Arman still be able to exhibit burnt pianos in picture galleries? How will César, who was unfortunately not in Paris in May to sign these cars, still be able to make "expansions" in public after that spontaneous expansion of thousands of students invading the Latin Quarter like a monstrous squirt from a giant tube of toothpaste?

Will the confrontation by the artists during the May Revolution turn out to be the beginning of a general reassessment of the artist's place in society, or merely a Poujadist expression of outdated professional demands?

If only the artist can realize that most of his output stamps him as a man of the past, an anachronism, this will be a great step forward. All he will then have to do is find out how he can become a man of the future. Or simply a man of the present, which would be an improvement.

The artist is a man of the past because he is prejudiced in favor of the unique work, of the artificial scarcity of his product so as to increase the price; he leans toward outmoded techniques like stained glass, ceramics, mosaics, tapestry, in a word, all fine craftsmanship. In many cases the artist seems an avatar of the artisan class. Soon, if he doesn't take care (but often he not only doesn't take care but takes pleasure in it) he will be the only artisan in a world that will finally have achieved its industrial revolution.

Henri Lefebvre is elated by the thought that the May Revolution was the first twentieth-century revolution, all those preceding it, including that of October 17, appearing in his eyes like nineteenth-century revolutions. The May Revolution revealed an aspiration toward the twenty-first century, since it struck violently against the bureaucratic centralism of Colbert and Napoleon I, since it proclaimed the necessity of reconciling socialism and liberty and rejected all dogmatisms in favor of permanent revolution. But it also revealed curiously outmoded tendencies, for its antitechnocratic manifestations often took on the aspect of anti-technological manifestations. The future belongs to automation, which alone can reduce the hours of work and thus release the worker from his oppressed condition, giving him access to culture and genuine leisure; and yet the nineteenth-century attack on the machine by the silk-weavers of Lyons has been revived by certain intellectuals who, to say the least, should give a little thought to economics and sociology before talking about Revolution. If the consumer society is to be condemned insofar as it becomes an end in itself, the absorption of the working classes into the consumer society thanks to mechanization and industrialization seems to me to be a form of progress that it would be monstrous to question under the pretext of Maoist Jansenism. To judge the consumer society in a country where the people do not consume is quite different from judging the consumer society in an industrialized country. Nor do they imply the same conclusions.

Furthermore, nineteenth-century vocabulary could be heard during the "events of May." For example, the "workers" are exalted at a time when there is no longer a leisure class; they are put on a pedestal at a time when they are in the process of becoming as anachronistic as the peasant (and the artist). It's not by chance that, for the moment, the only true beneficiaries of the May Revolution are the technicians and organizers, that is to say the men of the future.

The art of today not only delights in outmoded artisans' techniques, but also reveals a certain satisfaction in ugliness and anachronism. The artist is more inclined to express the ugliness of a world that is crumbling than the exaltation of a world that is being born. Most artists always give the impression of being present at a shipwreck.

Why do crafts rather than industry seem to hold the attention of contemporary artists? For example, many of today's sculptors betray in their work a romantic regret for a lost rural world where handmade implements, myths, and the sensuality of materials were fused in a pastoral community. Many sculptors produce work that is an echo of the lost world of shepherds and laborers, smiths and potters. Thus there is a whole vast tendency in contemporary sculpture to fall back on anachronistic popular folklore. The wine-press, the millstone, the workbench, the mortar, the cistern, the drinking-trough, the sundial, and the village fountain are among the elements contributing to their inspiration. Many contemporary sculptors seem to have read too much Giono in their youth without realizing that he has progressed in the course of years, passing from Virgil to Stendhal. Nevertheless, this still leaves us in the nineteenth century.

I fear that these outmoded artists are jumping on the confrontation bandwagon to challenge the industrial world.

To contend is fine; but to contend against what? And to contend with what gain in mind? The return to the soil, so dear to Pétain? The return to fine native materials and handicrafts? Let us beware of Poujadism!

Expressionism, dada, surrealism, lyric abstraction, and action painting have all been protests against the industrial revolution. All these schools have adopted a posture of rejection and withdrawal.

But expressionism must be viewed within the climate of its age, that is to say the years preceding the First World War. Expressionism was a presentiment of those appalling massacres, the cry of isolated men who feared technology, administration, the crowd, love. These "anarchists" were both liberated and disquieted by the "death of God" that Nietzsche had announced; wanting to be one with the humble, the poor, the proletariat on the march, they were torn between the "fabulous future" of Modern Times, which they had caught a glimpse of, and a romantic nostalgia for the past. Hence the only position they could take was one of rejection.

This rejection prompted them after the First World War to violently oppose the artist-engineers of the Bauhaus, who themselves were trying to infiltrate the decrepit structures of society in order to shatter them. In art, the twentieth century was born at Dessau and Weimar. This is so in spite of the fact that most of the Bauhaus painters were rather anachronistic easel painters. Only Moholy-Nagy and to a lesser extent Albers were aware of a new art that would father a new architecture conceived in the same places by Gropius, Breuer, and Mies van der Rohe.

Dada was total rejection.   The war of 1914-18 had left its debris and charnel-houses.   After the Second World War, Brasillach would say in despair, "We have nothing left but the black flag and our friends."   That was doubtless the conclusion arrived at by the Dadaists.   Then Surrealism tried to construct a new religion on the ruins of Dadaism, with a liturgy drawn from Gustave Moreau and Hieronymus Bosch.   The Surrealists were the children of Trotsky and Freud, and they were certainly antitechnological.   Their Polynesia was the occult, the dream, the disorder of the senses.   There was confrontation too, but confrontation by way of intellectual escape.   cf. B.

During the course of this century, which hasn't finished vomiting up its predecessor, can be found a whole line of outmoded confrontations, parallel with a whole line of forward-looking confrontations.   We were saying that in art the twentieth century was born in Dessau and Weimar with the Bauhaus, but it was conceived at the same time in Italy with Futurism, in Holland with *De Stijl*, in Russia with Constructivism, and in France with Delaunay and Léger.   All these movements aspired to the formulation of a poetics of technology and the creation of an art that would be an environment for all men at every moment of their lives, an art that would accompany them without their being aware of it.   This is how art will be truly socialized—that is, it will permeate everywhere.   It will be a part of man's conditioning.

But if outmoded confrontation can lead to Pétainism and Poujadism, the fascination of technology can lead to facism.   This was the case with Marinetti, who moved from the cult of the machine to the cult of force.

After the Second World War, lyric abstraction in Europe and action painting in the United States were understandable positions of withdrawal.   The artist was rejecting the exterior world in favor of his interior world, he made his own films and told his own stories.   Every lyric abstractionist lived in his Polynesia.

Then came Neo-dada, the New Realism, and Pop Art, which were not an art of total rejection like Dada, but rather an art of derision.   These three movements, begun in the spirit of confrontation, provide a perfect example of a "rejection" that has been taken over by the consumer society.   In a few years Arman, César, and Martial Raysse left the most outrageous confrontation to end up at the Hôtel Matignon in the collection of M. Pompidou.   By another route, the indomitable Marcel Duchamp saw certain of his anti-works cast in bronze and

31

thus become speculative works. Marcel Duchamp has had more time to find acceptance than Rauschenberg, but Rauschenberg too has found it. This may prove Marcuse to have been right.

The communist countries take art very seriously and consequently they mistrust it. They completely deprive it of freedom so as to put it in the service of the party. Jdanov believed that if liberty were allowed to art, this would be the equivalent of shaking the structure of socialist society. This places art very high and attributes to it more power than it actually has. Under the influence of Jdanovism, the young Czech painters who recently made their own cultural revolution were greatly disenchanted when they saw that though art had been de-Stalinized in their country, a general de-Stalinization of their society did not follow[2]. Jdanov had overestimated art. Whether Soviet painters are free to paint abstractly or figuratively tomorrow will not in any way change the fate of the Soviet Union.

Can it be that painting is only an art of pleasing ornamentation?

Contrary to orthodox communism, capitalism doesn't take art seriously; it lets artists do as they like, knowing full well that if it wants to it will survive even the most revolutionary somehow or other. Thus, one of the best lyric abstractionists, Pierre Soulages, has been adopted in spite of himself by the American consumer society, Gaullism, and the Communist Party. We learned from the press that in one and the same week Waldeck Rochet placed a Soulages tapestry in the room where a Communist Party congress was being held, while M. Georges Pompidou hung a picture by the same artist in his office, and American collectors, though both anti-Gaullist and anticommunist, continued to collect Soulages; this was the same Soulages who had the courage to make a poster attacking the American war in Vietnam and to sign all the revolutionary manifestos of the May uprising.

But what reason in there to think the consumer society in its various aspects, from the Prime Minister to the Leader of Her Majesty's Opposition, would not absorb Soulages when it has absorbed Che Guevara! Thank to posters, Che Guevara has, as we know, become an object of esthetic consumption like Brigitte Bardot. The same with the posters of the May Revolution. Collectors collect these posters made by students at the École des Beaux-Arts and by painters, even though one of the revolutionary objectives of these students and painters was to oppose by all possible means the world of collectors, dealers, and museums. The May Revolution's graffiti and slogans have been processed by bookstores and sold like any gadget.

Even the art of revolutionary propaganda can become, in less than a month, art of pleasing ornamentation.

To the question, "Can it be that painting is only an art of pleasing ornamentation?" we could add this second, even crueller question: "Can it be that painting is a tranquilizer?"

Matisse made it and article of faith. Did he not write: "My dream is of an art of balance, purity, and tranquility, without any disquieting or disturbing subject matter. For all who work with their brains, the businessman as well as the writer, for example, it must be soothing, a sedative, something analogous to a fine armchair that offers rest from physical fatigue."

Art considered as an armchair. Why not? But we are straying far from the May Revolution.

Far? Perhaps not, because the opposition was precisely to this soothing, tranquilizing art, this armchair art, which some people tend to consider as typically French art. In confronting the School of Paris, the schools of New York and London had this objection as their starting-point: French art is too comfortable.

The objection is unjust, for if the *fauve* Matisse roared like a sheep, his contemporary Rouault, who was a true Frenchman, didn't create a comfortable art but an art of confrontation in the manner of Léon Bloy, a Christian pamphleteering art in which the crucifixion had more place than the armchair. And as for Dubuffet and Fautrier, who are also true Frenchmen, haven't they produced an art of confrontation, bearing the same stamp as a Bacon in Britain and a de Kooning in the United States?

Let us leave the quarrels between the schools of Paris and New York, for they are nothing but well devised booby-traps set by the art dealers. The May Revolution has immersed us in a problem that is much more serious because it is much more real.

When the French students and intellectuals decided in the name of culture to shake the consumer society, that society replied with the utmost brutality: "When anyone speaks to me of culture I bring out my C.R.S." Thereupon the "intellectual revolution" was very quickly transformed into a "cultural revolution" in the Maoist manner, and the students in turn began to rise up against the culture and art that appeared to them as products of bourgeois society (of which they themselves were products).

The success was such that only the Minister of Cultural Affairs remained to defend culture and art. Now it is a strange fact that during the whole of the

33

"cultural revolution" André Malraux, the Minister of Culture, said nothing. The word "revolution" drew not a word from the mouth of the author of *Les Conquérants* and *L'Espoir*. The word culture apparently awoke no echo in the mind of the author of *Les Voix du Silence*. Indeed, during the events of May and June 1968, culture and art no longer seemed to interest anyone. Drawing the unavoidable conclusions, the museum curators closed their cemeteries of culture. Infected by this example, the private galleries locked their doors. A curious autodestruction of art and culture appeared, bringing to mind what Friedrich Hegel had written a hundred and fifty years before:

"Art, seen in relation to its supreme destination, remains a thing of the past. It has hence lost for us what once made it true and vital, its former reality and necessity."

During the May Revolution, the city once again became a center of games, it rediscovered its creative quality; there instinctively arose a socialization of art—the great permanent theater of the Odéon, the poster studio of the ex-École des Beaux-Arts, the bloody ballets of the C.R.S. and students, the open-air demonstrations and meetings, the public poetry of wall slogans, the dramatic reports by Europe No. 1 and Radio Luxembourg, the entire nation in a state of tension, intensive participation and, in the highest sense of the word, poetry. All this meant a dismissal of culture and art, doubtless because "official" culture and art were empty of any forward-looking content, because they had become arts of pleasing ornamentation. And within this term "official" must be included avant-garde and so-called avant-garde art since it has become official to the extent of being quoted on the stock exchange, collected by museums, Greek ship-owners, Nelson Rockefeller, Georges Pompidou, etc.

To be sure, art critics were attacked even more violently than artists; they were attacked not only by the students who attacked the artists but also by the artists themselves. But how many of these artists and students knew that at the General Assembly of AICA (the International Association of Art Critics) which was held at Venice in 1964, the question of the death of art had been widely discussed? The great international art critics who met in Venice expressed concern at seeing commerce risk the destruction of art to make money on artistic fashions that are as ephemeral as profitable—isn't it playing the consumer society's game to change fashions in art as often as possible, the way car models are changed to render them artificially outmoded? But apart from that, these critics expressed the opinion that art as usually understood was perhaps destined to disappear: it wasn't certain that the man of tomorrow would still need art.

34

This opinion is shared by a sociologist like Abraham Moles, who declared in 1965:

"Can it that we are at the end of a long period of questioning, trial, and experimentation which has reached the limit, a total destruction of artistic form?... The artist no longer struggles with his material, but with ideas—or with the administration. He's no longer uncertain about his life, but about the meaning of his life. He no longer makes works of art, he makes ideas for making works of art... He no longer decides; he experiments, rectifies, improves."

The death of art, or death of an art, of our art. Death of the art of rural civilization for the benefit of an art of urban civilization. Death of the art of the civilization of artisans for the benefit of an art of industrial civilization.

We are at a moment of rupture, a rupture that has been accentuated by the May Revolution, but which was already noticed as early as 1956 by Pierre Francastel when he wrote in *Art et Technique*:

"An art of our time exists. It has difficulty in penetrating the realm of everyday realities because it is in full growth—in the midst of a period of problemization—and also because a bad theory is retarding its encounter with the practical activities of the world of actuality. Science and art are the witnesses of a complete renewal of the forms of human life. One can't expect art alone to have reached the point of maturity."

Art is always the reflection of a given society. As the urban and industrial society is still in search of its identity, it's too much to demand that art should already reflect that society. Art is behaving like the post-rural, post-artisan society in which we are trying to live in the twentieth century: it's suffocating, it's dying of sclerosis, it's bursting into fragments. But we can have an inkling of what the art of a scientific society could be, the art of *homo ludens*, the art of a society that will have reconciled the concepts of socialism and liberty.

What the students condemned was the art of pleasing ornamentation dear to Henri Matisse. They demanded more from the artist than the manufacture of armchairs. Certain artists thought they were on the right road if they painted revolutionary pictures—against the war in Vietnam, against racism, etc. But this "political painting," exhibited in the salons alongside bouquets of flowers and landscapes, sold in galleries alongside abstractions, receiving prizes, and competing in Biennales appears to be a hoax.

Not that the artists are insincere, not that they doubt the effectiveness of their message, but this message is caught in a trap, being immediately taken over by the consumer society, which uses it as one of its ornaments. The great massacre at Guernica, which inspired Picasso to paint the picture everyone knows, now on permanent exhibition at The Museum of Modern Art in New York, doesn't arouse the indignation of American viewers toward similar massacres in Vietnam. Picasso's *Guernica* is regarded as a "masterpiece of art," nothing more. It has become an object of esthetic consumption. It isn't a political weapon, but a glorious picture. And it is one of the most precious possessions of any American museum.

If art is to be a means of effective confrontation with a lasting impact, it must escape from the limitations of the easel painting, from being a mere wall adornment. The political propaganda paintings on entire gable-end walls of apartment houses in Cuba have this impact. But they are part of the Cuban social system. They are the expression of it. They speak the same language as Fidel Castro or the sugar-cane cutter. There were similar Soviet paintings in the years immediately following the October Revolution, particularly the propaganda trains, which were entirely covered with revolutionary paintings, or the "environments" depicted on factory walls.

On the other hand, the social realism that came after this art of confrontation was a rediscovery by the socialist society of the formalism of bourgeois art. Just as the socialist State deemed that the people "had the right to marble columns" and threw a bit of them everywhere on its public buildings, just as it deemed that the people who used the subway every day "had a right to the pompous art of the aristocracy" and created a kind of outdated museum, this socialist State wanted to offer the people the art which bourgeois society reveled in, an orthodox, photographic art in the form of easel painting. Russian communism by some strange aberration conserved a bourgeois concept of art. In capitalist countries, social realism was an art of protest, for its purpose was to expose the vices of capitalist society, but in a socialist state it became soothing, its aim was to point out the virtues of that society. Both societies held fast to imagery and decoration. Although Russian communism deprived the visual arts of their speculative function, it preserved their character as precious objects to be placed in museums. The communist masses filed past these "masterpieces" as if before icons.

This was a situation as far removed from the socialization of art as in the capitalist countries. The only form of democratization arose from the fact that these "masterpieces" belonged to nobody. They were in some way "nationalized." But, as we know, the difference between nationalization and socialization is as fundamental as between management by officials and management by the workers.

One thing greatly surprised me in Czechoslovakia. I was told that the public was deprived of art in a socialist country because if the museums and corporate bodies bought works by modern artists there would be no works left for private ownership.

Here we find a strange persistence of the taste for individual ownership, for the picture to hang above the sideboard in the dining room. In fact, the artist and contemporary society should be of such a kind that the worker not have art in his home but that he live in art, that his house and place of work be works of art, that the streets be works of art, that the entire society bathe in art.

"The old classic humanism ended long ago, and ended badly," wrote Henri Lefebvre (*Le droit à la ville*). It is dead. The mummified, embalmed corpse weighs heavily and doesn't smell good. It occupies a lot of public space or else is transformed into cultural cemeteries in humanistic guise: museums, universities, various publications. Plus new housing projects and journals of town-planning. It provides a wrapping for trivialities and platitudes. "Human scale," people say—at a time when we must adopt something that is out of scale, something of the size of the universe.

It's this "something" that will be the art of tomorrow, if it manages to emerge from the ruins.

What at the moment is the esthetic element that brings life to our streets and roads and gives them a germ of poetic environment unless it is advertisements, mass art, sometimes art produced by teamwork? Without posters and neon lights our cities would be gray indeed. The architectural polychromism which architects talk about scarcely exists in fact, except empirically in advertising posters.

Will the front of the Citroen DS 19, not to mention the design of the Caravelle and the dresses of Courrèges, have less of a place in the history of contemporary forms than such and such contemporary sculpture exhibited with a great to-do in galleries and museums, a gratuitous form that alone qualifies for the label "work of art"?

Perhaps it is first and foremost the "work of art" that was aimed at in the confrontation. The work of art and not art. Each artist works at his own masterpiece in the way that craftsmen who wished to acquire their masterships formerly did. The masterpieces of these craftsmen were wonders of their kind, reproducing the forms of staircases, gates, and frames on a miniature scale.

Let us imagine making these masterpieces without ever progressing to the scale of the objects themselves, and we will be in somewhat the same situation as our artists. Each of them makes his wonderful staircase twenty centimeters high, his perfect piece of cabinet-work. During this time the housing developments are without staircases of the scale of real life.

Another comparison: when the first taxis appeared, they aroused the anger of the horse cabmen. However, some farsighted horse cabmen went to take their driving tests.

The artist as clown, the artist as hostage, the *artiste maudit* all run the risk of being as anachronistic as horse cabmen in the world of tomorrow unless they take heed of the inescapable changes in contemporary society.

The temptation of retreat is considerable. No one will deny that the contemporary world and that which one can conceive of the world of the future are not highly desirable. Nearly all contemporary artists have opted for retreat. Doubtless some workers and employees would do the same if their own alienation didn't necessitate their waiting for the appointed time of retirement. But the artists' alienation is flexible enough for them to benefit from all the privileges of the consumer society while adopting a comfortable attitude of rejecting that society. To really reject the consumer society would be to refuse to sell one's works and thus be reduced to taking another job than that of artist; this would demand that the artist socially alienate himself to make a living and hence be unable to enjoy his retreat. There's no way out.

Jean Dubuffet, who makes an article of faith out of confrontation and retreat, has written: "There's a close collusion between culture and the dealers." That is true. He goes on: "Culture and commerce march hand in hand. You will not destroy the one without destroying the other." Agreed.

But Dubuffet's position becomes confused when he adds: "The production of art is a highly individual function, and consequently quite opposed to any social function. It can only be an antisocial function, or at least asocial."

What it comes to is that Jean Dubuffet hasn't cut himself off from the world of culture, nor from that of the dealers. He is one of the privileged in the "production of art." He takes on a "social function" which is that of a famous painter, even if he's a revolutionary famous painter. Society accepts him very well as he is, hangs his works in museums, and pays high prices for them. And when in 1960 the Museum of Decorative Arts in Paris gave Jean Dubuffet a retrospective exhibition, the opening page of the catalog read: "The retrospective exhibition of works by Jean Dubuffet, under the high patronage of M. André

Malraux, Minister of State for Cultural Affairs, was opened by M. Gaëtan Picon, Director General of Arts and Letters."

The French Republic never did any more for Bonnat or any other of its archpriests. Jean Dubuffet could well write in his pamphlet *Asphyxiante culture*: "The State, as I see it, has only one face—that of the police. To my eyes all government departments have this single face and I can't imagine the ministry of culture as other than the police of culture, with its prefect and superintendents."

Nonetheless the fact remains that he has become absorbed by that minister, his prefect and superintendents and that he has even accepted their blessing.

Isn't retreat a form of imposture unless the break with society is complete? Gauguin himself, secluded in Polynesia, relied on Vollard for sales in order to subsist. And he pestered Daniel de Monfreid when the money from the sale of his pictures didn't reach Tahiti quickly enough. Thus Gauguin counted on the smooth funcioning of capitalist society to live in his retreat on Tahiti. Dubuffet at Saint Paul de Vence. Or Henry Miller at Big Sur. When all is said and done, these "anarchists" are just as dependent on the consumer society as those who play a part in the consumer society. What's more, they themselves play a part. They are its folklore. The consumer society dearly loves them. They are also its good conscience. Bourgeois society adjusts much better to a Gauguin in Tahiti than to a Courbet in the Place Vendôme.

---

1. The campus is a ghetto for students just as the Low Rent Housing Development is a ghetto for workers, the garden apartment a ghetto for supervisors, etc...

2. Finally it has followed.

André Fermigier

"No more Claudels"

During the months of May and June 1968, one half of France confronted the other—the street confronted the State, the crowds confronted the parties, children contested the authority of their parents, workers that of their employers and trade unions, youth confronted the world of adults and its system of values, students confronted their professors, and the professors, who had only been waiting for this opportunity, confronted each other.   Although the confrontation at times developed in an atmosphere of revolt and riot, to the accompaniment of missile-throwing and such other disturbances as were necessitated by resistance on the part of the contested authority and its representatives, it was not in principle a revolutionary activity.   Except for some points of detail ("No more Claudels" was written on the wall of the Sorbonne)[1], it didn't claim in a mechanical and immediate way to replace an old order by an antithetical, previously defined new order.   To say of a proposition that it is contestable doesn't imply that one considers it false at the point of departure; the politician who contests the results of an election appeals to a rational authority of arbitration, to a checking procedure that will establish what is right.   Thus to confront is to call for the opening of a dialogue, to reject the source of authority and the existing authorities, to recognize the validity of an institution or an idea only in terms of a debate between the interested parties.   A very old practice, as you can see, and one specifically French.

In the university, where everything began and to which everything will return, the confrontation arose less over the content of the culture than over the way it was distributed and over the order of importance established among its various elements.   It is difficult to contest the rules of indirect speech in Latin syntax. But—and this is the first point and one to which we shall come back—is there

41

any need to talk so much about indirect speech? The objection that students had to university culture, as it develops from the sixth grade in the lycée to the teachers' qualifying examination, was that it was a bourgeois culture, based on the benign humanism and moderatism of 1900, sacrificing everything to rhetoric and the reconciliation of opposites; it was boring, "old" ("Professors, you're making us old!"), it ignored life, love, poetry, and the dramatic or hateful reality of the actual world. In its wish to be apolitical, the university puts a brake on free expression, forbids discussion, and serves the material and moral interests of the governing class. What's more, and this is the second point, it constitutes a caste in itself; the proportion of workers' and peasants' sons is minimal in the universities and great schools ("in the universities, 6% are workers' sons, in the re-education institutes they are 90%"); the university has a mandarin attitude, with recruitment from within, etc... The third and last point: if, for the sake of argument, I am interested in the rules of indirect speech and have freely chosen to study them, not been forced to by an archaic curriculum, what proof is there that the instructor who will teach me is qualified to do so? None, except the authority he derives from his office. I challenge that authority because I have played no part in establishing it and also because experience has shown me that certain of these "masters" could be and were frivolous, lazy, slack in attendance, mediocre, incompetent, or worthless. Then let us modify the nature of the relationship between the teacher and the taught. Let us no longer tolerate a situation in which the teacher treats the student as a minor, directing him, excluding or including him as if he were a laying hen or a tomato plant, only bothering with him if he recognizes his own image in him. Let there be no more examinations, prize-winners, stars, and elite students. Culture must no longer be an aristocratic privilege accorded to a college of vestals whose job is to maintain a purely ritual orthodoxy. It must be offered to all, it must be made by all and for all. "Culture is dead. Create."

These are the guidelines, and the elements of them can be found more or less in most of the social and cultural groups that participated in the movement. And particularly in the field of architecture, both the practice and the teaching of it. The confrontation was especially viable and effective at the École des Beaux-Arts: the studios were dissolved, certain professors, mandarins, and department heads whose negligence and mediocrity were scandals of long standing were simply thrown out, and the Minister of Cultural Affairs finally confirmed the decision taken in the middle of May by the students themselves: to close the school. This was a decision that everyone knew was necessary, but which had always been put off for fear of offending powerful interests.   In fact since 1863 the reform of the École des Beaux-Arts had been under consideration, and the inadequacy of its teaching was generally held to be one of the principal reasons for France's feeble contribution to modern architecture. In the last thirty years, what professor at the École des Beaux-Arts has designed a building of incontestable quality and international standing?   Mediocre architects, even with the cachet of the *Prix de Rome*, can't shape students of a really high level, and the school's aim was to turn out "artists" in conventional limited series who thought in terms of designs, palaces and monuments, rather than genuine builders.   The May rebels were not mistaken when for the term architecture they substituted the more socially committed and deliberately more prosaic expression "act of building." Let me quote from a work by Maurice Besset to which the events of May have given a prophetic quality: "If there is scarcely a country in which art and architecture are free from difficulties in accommodating themselves to industrial civilization, these difficulties have been aggravated in France by several factors that have created a severe crisis out of what need only have been a passing sickness.   The inadequacy of the education received by the future architect is the best known of these factors...   The system of values that holds back the École des Beaux-Arts is composed of pretentious vulgarity and artful rhetoric; it keeps the students in a cultureless state from which few have the taste and the means to break away."[2]

But that isn't all, for "the monopoly in instruction is prolonged by a vast system of restricted fields.   Throughout the whole of his career the architect must count on the influence, whether official or concealed, of the heads of the school and its purest products, the *Prix de Rome*.   A small number of monstrously inflated agencies, whose directors are loaded with honors and remunerative functions and will hardly care to risk their jobs over the adventure of any kind of research, divert all the important programs in their own directions...   In the midst of a wave not only of intense activity in the field of construction but, above all, of a total rethinking of architectural forms, this privileged, mandarin regime reduces a good number of the better minds in French architecture to a state of semi-unemployment, or at best to undertaking odd jobs which don't allow them either financially or technically to research the problem in its proper dimensions."

To this must be added the responsibilities that are equally shared between the public and the private sector.   In the private sector, all building projects are in the hands of promoters who organize the abjectness of economically accessible housing with the one concern of immediate rentability and scoff at the idea of architectural research.   When it comes to the public sector, we need not even mention the often absurd restrictions imposed by administrative regulations; we know what kind of architects our ministries turn to, especially the Ministry of National Education, which has built more than any other in the last twenty years and yet hasn't more than three decently designed schools to its credit. Finally we must not forget "the public's uninformed state," "its surly mistrust of all novelty," "its acceptance of scandalous inadequacies in current production." Much could be said on the incurably bad taste of the French middle classes who, after wallowing in their suburban "cottages," take delight in ridiculous "residences," fitting them out like little farmhouses; all they dream of is replacing the plywood and wrought iron of the thirties with the fake marble, mahogany, gilded metal, and Babylonian entrance foyers of the new apartment houses in the sixteenth arrondissement.   Given this level, is it possible to speak of a clientele? The young rebel architects have repeatedly said that good architecture involves a dialogue between the man who builds the house or factory and the man who will live or work there.   At present this dialogue simply doesn't exist.   Delays in building schedules and the persistent housing crisis (a phenomenon unparalleled in Europe, so there must be some reasons for it) ensure that the buyer almost never participates in the "act of building"; he takes what he finds, mainly because he belongs to the "disadvantaged" classes, and an ill-planned, hideously decorated barracks, dormitory, or Low Rent Housing Development has become the fate of the majority of Frenchmen.   We know the results only too well—an incredibly mediocre level of performance, ancient cities and splendid landscapes forever disfigured, Sarcelles, Maine-Montparnasse, the Paris region engulfed in rubbish and a muddled traffic and transportation system.   The scandal has become so great that the public has become conscious of it.   There has never been so much talk about architecture and city planning as in the last year.   When the plans for renovating Les Halles were shown, the reactions from press and public were so negative that they had to be withdrawn.   Now the administration will have to wait for better days and think up others—which will probably be no better if the same architects are used.

All this has been said by the students of the École des Beaux-Arts, and one can imagine with what vigor.   Moreover the history of modern architecture from Loos to Gropius and Le Corbusier is one of permanent confrontation, particularly in a country like France, where the academic tradition is very strong and can pride itself on a relatively brilliant past, at least on the technical plane.   The originality of the confrontation of 1968 is that it was concerned less with forms than with structures. That our houses and schools are appallingly ugly, that France is still *the* country of the badly housed, is something the young architects and architectural students knew; but they did not seem very concerned about it—even to a point that sometimes struck me as a little disturbing. First of all, they sought a new definition of the place of the architect in society; they wanted to reform, to "defeudalize" as they put it, the profession by suppressing the system of program directors and studios, the *Prix de Rome*, financial administrators, and agencies that are entirely subservient to private interests and where creative work is impossible. The May revolutionaries also demanded the suppression of the architects' association and occupied its premises for some time in order to denounce "the incredible fact of its responsibility for the present antisocial and segregationist state of affairs in building construction and town and country planning since the liberation, all the actions it has taken or refused to take on behalf of the privileged class or by mediocrity" showing its "bourgeois approach."

That was the root of the problem, the main motive behind the confrontation. It's not enough to say that the architect is no longer a proudly isolated "artist," responsible to himself alone for his creation. It's no longer enough to recall that architecture and town-planning are closely related, to say with Shadrach Woods that "all our problems are problems of town-planning, that the primary concern is neither to create objects in space nor to enclose volumes... but to organize places for the development of the activities of the men of today and, in so far as our knowledge permits, of tomorrow." To be sure, it would be as well to take some urgent measures (including the municipalization of urban land) which the most far-seeing French town-planners have long demanded, particularly Michel Ecochard. But we must go further; architecture, more than being a particular sector of economic activity, is a "political act." Architecture is impossible in a country governed by speculation, the squandering of land, where "the inventory of social realities for all regions hasn't been made," where people still think only in terms of "fine" architecture and privileged sites with a bourgeois clientele in mind, the rest being huddled into planless areas. "No hut-cities or tin-can-cities" was the slogan at a meeting organized in June at the Mutualité by revolutionary architects. The first duty of the architect is to decline the role of "town-planner of social segregation" which he has been willing to play for twenty years.

In such a perspective, one can understand how the problem of forms seems of secondary importance. On the way to a lecture-room in the Sorbonne one could hear speakers on every side shouting, "That's all very well. We're occupying these places, we can do anything we want to. But what are we going to do? We don't know. Let's at least agree on a common program that's efficient and possible to achieve immediately. At the Sorbonne this program was never defined. At the École des Beaux-Arts the question of the program was not even raised (except perhaps in committees). In fact it wasn't necessary to try to impose solutions, but to wait until they arose with social spontaneity, with the formulation of the needs of all those who were concerned with the "act of building," that is to say the whole population, the users of buildings; yet until now no one ever dreamed of asking them for their opinion or encouraged them to be aware of what they want; also concerned are construction workers; not only should their scandalous working and living conditions be reformed (insecurity, underpaid foreign labor, etc...), but they should be called upon to participate in the common enterprise. If architecture tends more and more to be reduced to a mechanical activity, to the assembly of separate parts, if it is at this point insensitive and inhuman, it is because all those who should be making it rather than submitting to it, from the mason to the corporation architect, are themselves treated like separate pieces and mechanical elements. Is this medieval nostalgia, the sentimentality of a William Morris for the artisan? Perhaps, even if one may cite on this point the experience of Paul Bossard at Créteil, where "the system of prefabrication aims not only at an improvement in working conditions, security, and efficiency" but "at demanding intelligent work from the laborer in spite of the inevitable repetition of similar operations and at making him take an active part in carrying out a process whose spirit he must be taught to grasp." (Besset.) We find ourselves continually coming back to the ideas that were at the center of the "situationist" confrontation in May—to open a dialogue, to give a voice to everyone, to look for the solution to problems in the movement, creative vitality, and "imagination" of the many, to bring the individual star into the ranks, whether professor, artist, or "great painter," to abolish privileged positions and artistic and cultural hierarchies which only reflect "segregation" and social inequality.

The confrontation is clearly not limited to architecture, and we shall find it again in the field of "art" *par excellence*, that is to say painting, inspired by ideas that are analogous to those we have just described; but in painting there is a much more complex development because of the particular way in which it is made, seen, and sold today. In painting we don't find such a simple relationship, so clear an antagonism as that between teacher and pupil, between the maker and the consumer of architecture. Painting is a game with a larger number of participants—at least five: the painter, the dealer, the critic, the buyer (private collector or museum director) and the public. The roles of these five are of very unequal importance, and we can immediately eliminate one of them, even if he should logically be the most important. The participant who is of no consequence is the public. This is a characteristic of contemporary painting—it no longer has a public. Private views are society occasions, the Salons provide little family outings. The galleries and the museums of contemporary art are not—certainly not in France—visited by more than a coterie or an elite, whichever you prefer, of professionals, unless, of course, some sacred cow like Picasso is being exhibited. But the problem, as we shall see, remains the same; it's the mythic personality, not painting, that drew 800,000 visitors to the exhibition in November 1966. Art publications are almost always aggressively luxurious; their tone and price limit their circulation to a very restricted readership of initiates, or those who believe themselves to be such—snobs, semi-intellectuals and, at best, specialists. The public is indifferent or traumatized, and understandably so, if one thinks of the trash, infantile terrorism, and painful extravagances that have become the rule in painting during the last ten years; the public no longer takes part in the game except as completely passive crowds, more or less dragooned into "houses of culture" and revealing all the characteristics of a "cultural herd." How can we be surprised? In a bourgeois society and culture, painting can only be for a restricted few. If music today has a public, it owes it to the phonograph and the radio. Nothing of the sort exists in the field of painting, the means of information being virtually nonexistent; and it would be impossible to insist too strongly on the disastrous consequences of the total bankruptcy shown by our school and university programs of art education.

One may say that this has always been so. But is this true? It seems to me on the contrary that in the nineteenth century and the first years of the twentieth the public played a considerable role in the world of art. It was doubtless a bourgeois public, and it often called attention to its existence by protestations and lack of understanding that now strike us as shocking. But was this incomprehension more injurious than the "supercomprehension" of which painting is today the object and the victim? For this is the determining factor: scandal is no longer possible—the last that I have personally witnessed was the one provoked by the Picasso room at the 1944 Salon d'automne. For the last ten years it has been possible to exhibit anything, or simply nothing, say a white canvas, and present this piece of nothing as a work of art or a manifesto. No one will protest or object. It is thus all the more surprising that a fair amount of contemporary painting explores shock, aggression, the incommunicable message, and is based on the desire to astonish or violate the spectator. Just now I was speaking of Picasso, who to a large extent is responsible for this state of affairs. In 1933 a critic, in other respects stupidly reactionary, wrote as follows: "Picasso's entire work is based on this postulate, that the expression of a genius, no matter what language he has recourse to, is of necessity charged with genius. Now, it's true that the most magnificent discourse delivered in French before an audience of Papuans who are ignorant of our language perhaps remains, in itself, magnificent, but for them it will always be a dead letter. Or rather they can only be aware of a personal power, a human influx, a kind of mysterious electricity that emanates from the orator. Picasso has relied a great deal on this magic incantatory power." Yes, but at least he astonished, the critic grumbled, the public was furious, at least there was something of an uproar during the private views. Today: absolute silence. This proves there is no longer a public, or that the public finds its relation to contemporary art a colonial one, like so many "Papuans," or, to use a slightly vulgar expression which is unfortunately Dali's, like cuckolds.

Practically the same can be said about buyers as we have just said about the public, with the difference that the situation isn't new, and that since the end of the reign of the great art patrons the role of the buyer has never been decisive, except, of course, when it came to the heroic collectors at the end of the nineteenth century and the beginning of the twentieth. But are there still any heroic buyers? I'm afraid they are few compared with the speculators for whom pictures are signs of social prestige or generators of publicity, as in the case of industrialists, doctors, and large corporations, etc. The buyer's choice is nowadays almost always determined by the dealer, who acts as both artistic adviser and financier. And what about the museums? They can take part in the game; in the years after the war The Museum of Modern Art in New York certainly helped young American painters to feel their power and originality, while at the same time it informed and educated the public. As much cannot be said of the French museums, whose purchase and exhibition policies are nearly always passive; they have long honored none but the dead and the dying, and they confine themselves to apportioning their funds equitably among the various tendencies in contemporary art.

Three now remain in the lists—the painter, the dealer, and the critic; and I don't need to say how furiously they confronted each other during the great days of

May; the painter confronted the critic and the dealer, the critic confronted the dealer, as well as the laws and practices of the market; the dealers in some cases confronted each other but on the whole they prudently waited for better days. Everyone more or less confronted the State, its cultural powers and artistic policy. Finally—and this was perhaps the most important point in the debate—there was a confrontation with painting itself, both in its principles and in the kind that we see sold and practiced today.

As one might have expected, the critics were the most challenged and ill-treated of the three. Certain artists, and not always the best ones, unleashed themselves against these hangmen, these boors from whom comes every evil. I have been told of painters' meetings which critics were not allowed to attend. Painters have accused the critics of doing their job badly, of understanding nothing, of being idle, hasty, lightweight, biased, incompetent, stupid, and corrupt. That is not necessarily imprecise or even excessive. It is true that in comparison with former times the critic wields enormous power beside which the professor's or examiner's is nothing. Also he takes advantage of a privileged status in mistakes or in a material or intellectual dishonesty which with good reason can exasperate certain painters. To have to deal tactfully with an imbecile, to court someone who is worthy only of scorn, sometimes even to have to bribe him, is an unenviable situation; the discredit into which the art critic has fallen is something that needs to be stated, and it must also be stated that his average level is inferior to that of the literary or film critic. And yet dare I put up a defense of the critic, though I myself profess to be one? Yes. Some critics (very few, I can sincerely say) are of a more than dubious morality, and in our profession there are certainly no fewer dotards, seedy little thrusters and oracular nonentities than in other areas of the press and publishing. But why should the undignified behavior of a few be made into a characteristic of all? What has perhaps been most damaging to the art critic is the prodigious gobbledygook that with him takes the place of a vocabulary; and the prefaces to exhibition catalogs in particular would provide a classic anthology of the art of saying nothing. But even there, is it entirely the critic's fault? Confronted with a work that says nothing to you and about which there is nothing to say, what can you do except have recourse to jargon? There is clearly another solution, namely to say what you think, and the main objection that can be held against the critic is that he so rarely accepts his responsibilities, that he lacks intellectual courage, and that he scarcely ever dares say no; that would involve risks, and no risks are run by the critic who claims to be objective and is usually only passive,

49

prudent, and foolishly complimentary.   Many critics live in terror of missing the last train, of being behind the fashion or of repeating the mistakes of their confreres of 1880 and 1910.   This is the most honorable explanation that can be given of that paralysis which is so frequent in criticism today.   There are others that I would prefer not to dwell upon, but even there it seems to me that painters don't help the critics in their task by so often considering them (partially because of the difference in income) as nothing but hirelings.   The fawning critic is the object of undying rage and rancor if he allows himself the least bit of reserve.   *Genus irritabile vatum*!   And yet a critic has never been known to make (or unmake) an artist unless he is the instrument of a dealer.

We now reach the heart of the problem—the dealer and the art market. Everything has been said on the subject, and I refer in particular to the recently published book by Raymonde Moulin.[3]   Painters and critics have come together again to deplore a situation that truly is deplorable.   We know that in the case of all except the really great painters, the dealer is today the actual master of artistic life; it is he who makes and unmakes reputations, creates fashions, raises and lower prices; very often the reputation, even posthumously, of an artist depends, for better or worse, on the ability of his dealer to defend him.   We know about the scandalous profits of certain dealers, their wiles, their objectionable procedures and the extortionate contracts they impose on painters, citing the risks they run and the cost of publicity.   We know about their miserliness and greed, their way of breaking a commitment or losing interest in an artist when he no longer seems profitable to them.   Let us beware of generalizing: there are dealers who are admirable in their sincerity and unselfishness, dealers who are honest and courageous, dealers whose convictions can be respected even when one doesn't share them; and Raymonde Moulin has made it clear that the taste for money isn't peculiar to the dealer, and in his relations with painters the faults are not necessarily all on his side.   The entire system is awry, especially since the boom of the fifties.   The fact still remains that the prospect offered by the art market is one of the least inviting and most depressing that a person of sensibility can contemplate.   But what is the answer? Abolish galleries, as some have proposed?   What would replace them?   Authorized fixing of prices according to the age and importance of the painter?   One can scarcely see painters becoming civil servants, and who will grade them in order of rank?   An academy, an assembly of painters?   That smacks of Aristophanes, or else is an unpleasant reminder of what we know of the situation of the arts and painters in the socialist democracies.   One could of course demand that prizes and international competitions be abolished, one could attack the Biennales and insist that the State increase its aid to artists and make them all beneficiaries of the "one per cent rule." All? Even so, would these measures, and others besides, fundamentally change the situation?

The picture market by its very nature is unpredictable. All commercial transactions, all production rest on the sale of a raw material that is transformed into energy, capitalizing an established value in accordance with rules almost stable in terms of needs and the relation between supply and demand. The exception is in the case of cultural goods, particularly painting, and most of all contemporary painting. *Objets d'art* are precious in themselves; architecture is an industry, one among the various sectors of the economy; the price of old paintings is almost always guaranteed by time. But what about a picture painted in 1965? This is no longer a matter of consumption or capitalization but of pleasure and prestige, elements which are not open to precise evaluation; above all it is a matter of placing a formidable bet against the fluctuations of a market which revealed how vulnerable it was in the crisis of 1962. Pictures, ultimately speaking, are worth nothing; they can only be beyond price, in every sense of the term. Hence they give rise to the craziest market of imaginary values that has ever existed. Hence the sanctification of painting, aided by the cultural mythomania of the age. Hence, on the economic level, the image of the great painter as a kind of Midas, capable of "changing everything he touches into gold," as a *Paris Match* journalist wrote in 1950 apropos of Picasso. Hence arises a world of masters and slaves in which the harshness of economic laws and the whim of fashion aggravate the anxiety natural to every creator; even the greatest have to be constantly on their guard, and who can blame them? A single false step may be fatal. Nowadays painting can only provide a living in terms of absolute success. You win or you lose. *Aut Caesar aut nihil.* Painting is *the* world of Caesarism and the inequality of conditions.

The situation we have just been describing has been denounced so many times that the events of May, in spite of the extraordinary commotion they provoked in the world of art, do not strike me as having introduced any really new elements into the record of confrontation as regards painting, artistic individualism, and its economic and cultural consequences. Pop Art once again evoked the possibility of a collective, impersonal art,[4] or so people said, in spite of the unfortunate precedent set by socialist realism; it brought out the necessity of putting art in the service of the people, and this was done with great courage and conviction in the studio for the production of revolutionary posters that existed for some weeks at the École des Beaux-Arts. Some of these posters (particularly the anonymous ones that were not made by painters) are of an astonishing crudity and effectiveness; we saw them for a long time on the walls of Paris, with a look of poverty about them, for they were made with whatever means came to hand; they are primitive in the best sense of the word, translating the anger and hope of May with such spontaneity that they can be compared to the posters of the Russian Revolution, while they seem to reduce the "Dove of Peace" to the proportions of a fairly conventional work of art. But apart from these posters there was nothing that had not more or less been said before. Consider how much has been done in the last fifty years to "devaluate" painting! First there were the cubist collages, iconoclastic works about which Aragon wrote: "Painting turns to what is comfortable, it flatters the man of taste who has paid for it. It's a thing of luxury. A picture is a jewel. Now here is a way for painters to become free. Collage is young. It will be considered of no value for a long time to come. The general opinion is that collages can be reproduced at will. Everyone believes he can do something just as good. And if painters by a continuous act of will can perpetuate and aggravate the discredit into which they are fallen, they will perhaps be able to reach the point where... their works are no longer worth anything at all, absolutely nothing at all to people who consider they have the right to adorn their walls with human thought, with living thought, reviving those decorative panels of slaves that are scarcely seen nowadays outside the Folies-Bergères."[5] This passage was written in 1930. We know what has happened since.

There were also Duchamp's "ready-mades," and we may observe in passing that the "ready-made" finally realized its revolutionary potential when it took the form of paving-stones which the students threw at the C.R.S.[6] Today, ready-mades are in museums and have inspired volumes of esthetic commentary. There followed anti-art (which sells very well), the promotion of rubbish, *l'art autre*, and *l'art brut*. Finally there were serigraphs (an interesting experience) and multiples, but we shall reserve judgment on this last point; multiples under their existing copyright only seem to act as a cloak for a particularly astute commercial operation.

We are told that painting is dead, just as we were told in the nineteenth century that "God is dead," which today is no longer looked upon as a misfortune (and is something, moreover, which I personally regret). It's as old as the world, or rather as old as the moment when our world began to grow old, to prophesy the end of the world with Spengler and *The Decline of the West*, in

LA POLICE S'AFFICHE
AUX BEAUX ARTS

LES BEAUX ARTS
AFFICHENT dans la RUE

34

Atelier Populaire,
La Police s'affiche aux Beaux Arts,
Les Beaux Arts affichent dans la Rue, 1968

ATELIER
POPULAIRE

which we can read how decadence began with Wagner and Manet, whose art is "an obvious return to the elementary in opposition to the substantial painting and absolute music that preceded them... it signifies a gratuitous concession to the barbarity of the great cities and to incipient dissolution, and is concretely expressed in a combination of brutality and refinement." It's an "artificial" art tha "marks the end, it's incapable of any organic development. Hence it follows—what a bitter thought!—that the end of the fine arts in the West has been irrevocably proclaimed. The crisis of the nineteenth century was its death struggle. Faustian art dies of senility, like Apollonian and Egyptian art, like all the others after they have realized the last potentialities within them and have fulfilled their vocation within the living course of culture." To be sure, this "bitter thought" is formulated in particularly stupid terms. But the important thing is that it was formulated, and there is doubtless more sense to be found, more relation to some concerns of the moment, in these words written by Elie Faure in 1932 in an article entitled "The Agony of Painting": "Haven't I said that the easel picture should render, to the great art from which it derived, the homage of disappearing as quickly as possible so as to return to the comforting impersonality of being an auxiliary to architecture; and that the art of Matisse and Picasso led us to envisage the object no longer in terms of individual sentiment but of collective interest?" Hasn't he in fact said that painting must become "a language of the present, accessible to all, a kind of writing and... give up the role of an imperial art that it has been playing for three hundred years and particularly in the last century."[7]

It would be possible to multiply these quotations, to analyze the convergence of the interpretations of popular art, primitive art, naive art, paintings by children and the mentally deranged, to remember the importance attached to graffiti, the injunctions given to painters in 1945 to abandon the easel picture and return to the fresco, to impersonal decoration, to cling to the "wall."[8] The nostalgia for a collective and impersonal art, for a language of the present, for writing that is accessible to all has become a commonplace in criticism in the last thirty years. This is why there has been recourse to the dream, automatic writing, and the urbane and erotic pathology of the surrealists. "Language is a social fact, but can't we hope that one day the pictorial arts, like language, like writing, will be so too and that they too will pass from the social to the universal... It only remains for the human conscience to rebel against whatever tries to make it believe it's not an entirety, so as to end the outrageous inequality that obliges it to use philosophers and poets in order to take itself seriously, wrote Eluard in

"Donner à voir." He never tires of repeating, in the words of Lautréamont, that "poetry must be for everyone, not for an individual." If we look at it in this perspective, painting can only be conceived as "a sum of destructions," to use Picasso's phrase. The decisive moment, the culminating point in this evolution, came one day in 1918 when Casimir Malevich exhibited a picture entitled "White square on a white ground," which is in fact nothing but a white square on a white ground, hence nothing on nothing. As a visual expression of the Russian nihilism of 1900, this "white square on a white ground" allowed Malevich to undergo the pure experience of a "world without objects," to restore man to his original unity with the all, to discover a kind of "inverted sacredness," as Dora Vallier said, to get rid of art once and for all: "In the vast space of cosmic repose I have attained the white world of the absence of objects which is the manifestation of revealed nothingness."[9]

This mystic nihilism will still seem consoling and full of hope if we compare it with what some of our young painters profess and practice. In 1967 four of them (Buren, Mosset, Parmentier, and Toroni) organized a series of spectacles at which they said nothing, maintained an obstinate and indecipherable silence, showed canvases that each signed with the name of another and that were based on the repetition of an anonymous motif; their intention was to show the possibility of eliminating expression entirely; for Buren it was a strictly identical series of window-shade canvases mounted on stretchers. That is something that goes even further than "revealed nothingness." Daniel Buren explained his intentions and those of his companions in a highly interesting interview with Georges Boudaille, published in *Lettres Françaises* on May 13, 1968. I shall quote this at some length because it seems to me to sum up with great conviction and a remarkable feeling for the absurd all those variations on the theme of the death of art that we have been able to read for some years and which were often echoed upon the walls of the Sorbonne. The interview appeared some time after the publication of an article by Harold Rosenberg in whcich he declared that "the history of art is drawing to a close." Daniel Buren said he agreed with Rosenberg, but he immediately attacked Marcel Duchamp, whose influence, nonetheless, is known to have been considerable on painting and terrorist criticism in the last few years. We are faced with something that goes much further than Dada and the ready-made. "Duchamp realized there was something false about art, but he ended by increasing this instead of demystifying it. By appropriating the manufactured article and putting it outside its context he purely and simply symbolized art." The artist's crime is "to emasculate the observer, to impose his own anxiety, his own vision of the world… to claim the right of making you see what you can see for yourself and what you would be able to see much more accurately without his intervention… To think and say that there were no London mists before Turner is very pretty, very poetic; but it is outrageous. It is an attack on individual liberty. It is forcing another to have the same dream as you have. It was thus that after having seen Cézanne I became one of those mental prisoners who believe they *see* the mountain Sainte Victoire in the way he depicted it. I believed 'in' art. When I lost my faith, I realized that the mountain had disappeared. I finally saw the mountain Sainte Victoire. Art twists things; it stops you from realizing things as they are." In this respect Duchamp must bear more blame than Cézanne, for Cézanne has only "made icons" out of a limited number of motifs and visual experiences, while Duchamp, as soon as he "exhibits" a bottlerack, a spade, or a urinal, asserted "that anything whatsoever is art from the moment when it is taken out of its context, or when you point at it with your finger," or when he himself, Marcel Duchamp, with senseless pride, "made an icon" of it and pointed to it as a work of art. In a word, "To the extent that people express themselves for others by means of the visual arts, they will never be able to emerge from the realm of illusion because the created work will always be an expressive screen onto which any projected form whatsoever will appear in the form of an illusion of itself."

The solution? "To eliminate illusion of all kinds (including abstract illusion), esthetics, sensibility, individual expression, which doesn't mean that the answer is to work in a group, but that the work must become real, thought in the raw, and hence anonymous. I insist on the elimination of expression… the creation of something totally unconnected with what precedes it, into which the latter has put nothing, and thus something that expresses itself by nothing. Then artistic communication is broken. The thing presented no longer has any function, whether esthetic, moral, or commercial… The viewer finds himself alone with himself, confronted by an anonymous thing that provides him with no solution. Art is no longer there. It's a question of *something else*." Hence the window-shade canvas indefinitely repeated, the repetition being the best means of emptying the work of all emotional or intellectual content. Thus the artist will disappear at the same time as art, and in the process he will restore to everyone full responsibility for his relationship with the world. "Art is dead," said an inscription on the Sorbonne, "let's liberate our day-to-day life." "Poetry is in the street."

The death of art means that the power of creation is restored to everyone.

"Long live the creative masses. Say no to bourgeois non-culture," wrote one student, and another, quoting Benjamin Péret: "Art doesn't exist. Art is you." In his *Treatise on how to live in the manner of the younger generation*, Raoul Vaneigem said that "the capitalist system and its sequels are forced to compensate by means of consumption for whatever they lose in production... As man liberates himself from his function as a producer, he must dedicate his time to a new function, that of consumer. The worthy apostles of humanism offer the vague territory of leisure that has finally been made possible by the cut in working hours, but in fact they only raise an army ready to maneuver in the field of the consumer economy." What it amounts to is that everyone nowadays throws away his liberty to create, without becoming integrated in a system of mechanical production which was formerly the exclusive privilege of the artist. Vaneigem quoted Dewitt Peters as having declared "with touching candor... that if people were given colors, brushes, and canvas to amuse themselves with, something surprising might emerge." And Vaneigem added: "If this policy is applied in ten well-regulated fields like the theater, painting, music, writing, there will be some chance of giving people an artist's awareness, the awareness of a man whose profession is to exhibit his creativity in the museums and the shop windows of culture." And it is true enough that "the more a culture becomes a culture of the people, the more this means an increase in power." But "can we really believe that when men become aware of their creative force they are going to paint the walls of their prison and leave it at that?" Artistic spontaneity must be identified with revolutionary spontaneity, with revolutionary "creativity." "The search for new means of communication, far from being open only to painters and poets, now needs a collective effort. Thus the old specialization called art comes to an end. There is no longer an artist, for all are artists... There is no longer a work of art, in the classic sense of the term," since "the consumer society reduces art to a variety of consumable products... which makes demands of the utmost crudity. It is no longer possible to have a work of art under such circumstances, and this is all to the good. Poetry is elsewhere, in the event that is created... The future work of art will be the creation of an impassioned life."

It is possible to imagine gradations of opinion, less radical in their optimism (Vaneigem) or negation (Buren), those for example that Dubuffet defends in a recent and timely little work, *Asphyxiante culture*. Culture, insofar as it kills "creativity," is responsible for the crisis in today's art and civilization. Cultural mandarins arbitrarily divide the world between what is cultural and what is not, they divide men between the unworthy and those who have the right to culture, in the form of consumption and production. "Culture nowadays tends to have the place that was formerly given to religion. Like religion, culture now has its priests, prophets, saints, and college of dignitaries." It is in the name of culture that crusades are undertaken... that the western world justifies its appetites by its urgency to make Shakespeare and Molière known to the black nations." To be sure, this culture nowadays claims to be directed at the people, but it carefully keeps them at a distance: "The propertied caste, together with its learned helpers, opens its castles, museums, and libraries to the public, but—and let us make no mistake about this—it doesn't attempt to give the public the idea that they in their turn should dedicate themselves to creation. It isn't writers and artists that the propertied class intends to help by its cultural propaganda, but lecturers and administrators. Indeed, cultural propaganda deliberately makes the administered feel the abyss that divides them from those prestigious treasures to which the ruling class has the key; it also makes them feel the pointlessness of aiming at any worthwhile creative work outside the paths indicated to it."

Hence the amazing sterility of contemporary art, which contrasts with the superabundance of culture that has been thrust upon us. *Panem et circenses*. What in fact can man do with all these blessings if he has no means of using them? They are a mere circus act for those who are without the key of knowledge or a minumum of artistic education and information. Now, culture is the opposite of education, and we may even say that in France there has been no let-up in the attempt to compensate by means of cultural follies for the atrophy and progressive collapse of our educational system. It was Malraux, I think, who said that access to a work of art depends essentially on revelation, not on comprehension. All revelation presupposes an elect and, as Dubuffet said, prophets and a church. Culture makes no call upon creativity—artists are rarely cultivated men and cultivated men tend rather to be professors or *minores* than really artists; and not only that, but culture doesn't even invite participation, being founded on respect, nostalgia, apprehension, and terror. I shall not insist on the profoundly lugubrious and discouraging character of culture as defined in *The Voices of Silence* and *The Lighthouses*: "the evening when Rembrandt is still drawing and all the illustrious Shades and those of the cave painters watch the hesitant hand that prepares their new survival and their new sleep." Artistic activity is not necessarily to be identified with perpetually pulling out one's tie before destiny. I simply mean that there is no use in luring people to museums if they haven't the means of arriving at a true understanding, at a personal experience of works of art. The majority haven't these means. We find here again our cultural herd. What sight could be more heart-breaking than those haggard crowds that plod through museums, jostling each other in front of the *Mona Lisa*, photographing little girls in front of cathedrals, "doing" Italy in three days, following a guide around frightful châteaux? Culture has become a subdivision of tourism and gastronomy. People look at works of art the way they used to watch queens ride through the streets.

The detestation of culture strikes me as having been one of the dominant traits in May 1968. Not that anyone wanted to be iconoclastic or barbaric; no one proposed burning the libraries. But culture was identified with the bourgeoisie, with a class ideology, or, in a more immediate way, with that odor of boredom, of aggresive and bigoted mediocrity so often emitted by French universities, as from some stale, watered-down soup. Is it still possible to speak of "watchdogs," as in the time of Nizan? Perhaps, but never have beasts looked so mangy, never have privileged beings had so sad and famished a countenance. "Culture is the inverse of life," wrote the students. "Culture is dead. Create!"

Culture, said Dubuffet, can only produce "the cultured," telling their beads before the high priests. It has also been said that the university by its selection, competitive examinations, and Malthusianism can only produce intellectual and social mandarins. Esthetic individualism is aggravated by a market system whose sole aim is to produce "sacred cows" who are the source of immense profits, and results in artistic Caesarism and a lessening of creativity.[10] In the nineteenth century there was still a kind of pictorial artisan who was anchored in a sane, modest tradition; he was a painter of average quality who was very close to his consumers; he integrated himself spontaneously with their lives and he satisfied their wants. Painting of this kind no longer exists (or can no longer sell). Painting is locked in a Valhalla, largely through the fault of cultural myths, through the fault of a dramatic convention that carefully divides the main actors from the extras. "It is the power of the hierarchically structured Church of former times that state control intends to give to culture—in a vertical, pyramidally structured form. It is in quite the opposite way, in the form of horizontal proliferation, in infinitely diversified expansion, that creative thought would acquire strength and health. There is no greater obstacle to this proliferation than the prestige of certain show-offs who have been catapulted into the ranks of the great... Nothing can be more damaging than this, or more apt to deter the ordinary man from thinking for himself and to make him entirely lose confidence in his own abilities." And here finally is a passage in which "the thought of President Mao" seems reflected by the events of May: "Instead of nourishing the primordial swarm, the fertile mold from which grow a thousand flowers, cultural propaganda sterilizes them; instead it plants four hydrangeas made of colored paper of which it is very proud and at the same time it carefully uproots everything around them."

Can it be that "*art brut*" is this "primordial swarm"? What we have seen of it must leave us a little skeptical. This is still more the case with the various attempts that have been made to restore life to painting by means of mass culture (folk culture, as they say in America), the world of publicity, neon signs, comic strips, the products of the consumer society and the refuse of urban civilization. The result rarely seems to rise above the level of the gadget or reveal more ability than we see in the window-dresser or the fashion artist. And all this takes place in an atmosphere of the most pretentious snobbery and amidst an incredible fever of publicity. What's more, these works sell very well, are in the hands of excellent dealers and end up in the apartments of bankers and women of fashion. Is culture really so much to blame? Shouldn't the blame rest rather with those who, instead of organizing education, make it both within reach and inaccessible? Dubuffet burst out as follows against the Ministry of Culture: "The First Ministry of Information was founded in England during the war at a moment when it seemed expedient to falsify information... The first Ministry of Culture was founded in France a few years ago and it has already had the desired effect: to supplant free culture by a false substitute which will act like an antibiotic, occupying the entire place without leaving the smallest corner where anything else could flourish." Without forgetting the fact that controlled information is not an English invention but Hitler's, which Dubuffet perhaps had his reasons to forget, one would like to reply that if the entire place is occupied, it is because there is no one else to occupy it. We can't blame culture for the present crisis in painting (which is an international one), for painting has long been "decultured." And if anyone is to be blamed in this matter, it is certainly not our poor Ministry of Cultural Affairs, which doesn't exist. The important thing, said Dubuffet, is to be "against." But in the realm of the arts I really don't see *against* what or *against* whom we could still fight, revolt, or organize invective or secession since we are at zero. No more Claudels? By all means. A law against performing *L'Annonce faite à Marie* is something I could contemplate with enthusiasm, and if I learned that all Braque's works of the years 1907 to 1914 had just been destroyed, I should weep, I should wear mourning, but only a token mourning, and I would come to reconcile myself to the situation—on condition that these relics, in spite of their venerability, are not exchanged for shabby happenings or some frightful little painter or other whom I see elbowing his way so ungraciously to the front rank of the new generation. It was everywhere being said at the end of the eighteenth century that poetry was dead because it corresponded to an archaic stage in the evolution of mankind (the age of myths, fables, dreams, and gods) and that scientific rationalism, which had become the model for intellectual activity and the prescribed means of expression, had superseded it. It would have been wiser to have simply said that the poets of the age were extremely mediocre. It's not art that is now in the process of dying; it's rather that artists of talent, if I dare use so prosaic and old-fashioned an expression, are scarce, and I should like to repeat what Gide said in 1945: "The world will be saved by a few."

The sweeping return of primitivism and barbarous thought and the ideological void in which we live have led some to a nostalgia for the kind of creation in which nature and culture are reconciled, in which we can all rediscover ourselves, not on the plane of what is seen but what is lived—that "festivity" with which Raoul Vaneigem identified revolution. But Paris isn't Cuba, and Michel Leiris has pointed out to us that the African sculptor too is an artist and was regarded and valued as such. Besides, this isn't the West's first quarrel with images; the Cistercians and Franciscans in their early stages and above all the Reformation were far more violent and effective in their iconoclasm. Even so, images didn't disappear. There is doubless little hope nowadays for painting, in view of what has become of it in the last few years. Perhaps painters will arise in the future. Meanwhile all we can do is entrust art into the hands of architecture which can still say all that is to be said if it avails itself of the means.

September 1968

1. All the phrases is quotation marks without any reference to an author are from inscriptions on the walls of the Sorbonne and other university establishments.
2. Maurice Besset, *Nouvelle architecture française*, Niggli (Teufen, Switzerland), 1967.
3. Raymonde Moulin, *Le marché de la peinture en France*, Pauvert, 1967.
4. Pop Art would seem rather to offer homage to the products and myths of the consumer society. But in a way it adheres to an impersonal and anonymous art. This is what G.R. Swenson wrote concerning Andy Warhol: "The art critic has generally refused to admit that an object may be

the equivalent of an esthetic feeling, particularly if that object carried a trademark. However, abstract art is in a way a sort of object that we can identify with the particular sensibility of an artist. Andy Warhol presents us with objects in which we can see the exparession of the artist's collective, public sensibility. Many people are troubled by the process of depersonalization that characterizes today's art. They fear that this process is the expression of the constraints of a technological society. A good proportion of what is worthwhile in our lives lies in what is public, in what we share with everyone. These are the most current clichés, the most trivial banalities of our civilization, and we must reckon with them if we want to utilize what is still offered to us by this brave new world which is ultimately not at all without hope." Quoted by Lucy R. LIPPARD, *Pop Art*, Thames and Hudson, 1966.

5. Louis ARAGON, "La peinture au défi" (1930). Reprinted in: ARAGON, *Les Collages*, Collection Miroirs de l'Art, Hermann, 1966.

6. "The most beautiful sculpture in the world is a paving-stone, the heavy paving-stone thrown in a policeman's face."

7. Élie FAURE, *Agonie de la peinture. L'Amour de l'Art*, 1932.

8. The only concern in the years 1945-50 was to depersonalize and "decommercialize" painting. Hence the importance attached to mural decoration, tapestry, etc...

9. On Malevich and the analysis of his great critical theory, *Suprematism, or the world without objects*, read Dora Vallier's *L'Art abstrait*, Le Livre de poche illustré, 1968.

10. This rejection of virtuosity and individual creativity is equally clear in music, as can be seen by reading an article by Robert Siohan concerning a concert given by Stockhausen at the Darmstadt Festival: "Instead of a specially arranged concert hall, it's the entire house that's given over to music, the public being invited to wander or to remain at will in any of five different rooms that are, from the acoustic point of view, isolated. In four of these rooms are instrumentalists... who usually don't play separate pieces set down on paper, but produce sounds that could called raw material, and these are used by the coordinators in their different sections to effect combinations... When Stockhausen writes music he doesn't consider himself, properly speaking, as a creator but as a mediator between impulses emanating from universal forces and the mass of his listeners... It was with a similar idea in mind that he asked twelve composers to provide him with the material from which he hoped to create a collective work." (Robert SIOHAN, "Une bien curieuse expérience au Festival de Darmstadt," *Le Monde*, September 11, 1968).

Gilbert Lascault

Contemporary art and the "old mole"

The gap

The primary task of the artist is to destroy, to suppress; the rest is, at the most, addenda.   In any event, "what is negative—destruction—can be decreed; what is positive—construction—cannot.   That is virgin territory, with problems by the thousand.   Only experience is able to make corrections and open up new paths. Only a life that is in ferment and unshackled engages in a thousand new forms. It improvises, receives 'creative energy,' and corrects its own mistakes."[1]   A systematic optimism, whether intended or unintended, makes it possible to confront the danger, anguish, and sorrow of negativity and to take control of it. A work may be said to be of the present time when its effect on our sensibility is sufficiently all-pervading.   It stirs us, shakes us.   We immediately feel we are attacked.   And whether we like it or not, whether we are disarmed or not, our way of life is shaken and we lose our assurance.   We can interrogate the work. The work itself asks us questions and makes us question ourselves; it is constructed like a question.   It denies what has preceded it, it denies the other works around it; it questions its own meaning.   With good or bad conscience it questions the existing culture of which it is supposed to be a part.   The artist who is truly a witness to his age is not Bernard Buffet, or Brayer who painted the coronation of the Shah; it is the man who sees *how* the ground[2] of our present culture is crumbling and caving in, and who desires this collapse and expresses it.   The myths of the western world imitate those buildings that buckle and sway in Pol Bury's serigraphs.   Our society and culture, like our being, resemble the houses in Quito that Henri Michaux talks about; they are built on six meters of shallow land and thirty meters of precipice.[3]   More than at any other time in its history, art today depicts the abyss as it widens.   It brings on giddiness.   Works of art can advocate (only advocate, not produce) an eventual change in culture and society; they would never know how to submit to a reassuring "socialist realism"; they don't sing the pure glory of "positive heroes." They aid and abet negativity.

As Michaux wrote in a work significantly entitled *I was Born Dilapidated*: "I'm built on a missing column."[4] Contemporary art that takes the place of painting and sculpture in former times—without accepting that distinction—is obsessed by this void, this absence. Far from trying to hide it, art is revealing it at a time when it can't yet be analyzed in clear terms by coherent reasoning. It perceives and reveals a gap that proves to be the center and foundation of what we only call our *being* by a habit of thought, perhaps through conceptual laziness, so as to avoid feeling dizzy.

The exhibition *Documenta 4* at Kassel made it possible to understand this chasm in its various aspects.[5] The Bulgarian Christo has gone to the extreme in bringing us face to face with an immense empty room on which a glass door closes; confined, deserted, uninhabited, perhaps uninhabitable, in any case irremediably inaccessible. Fontana's torn, split, gaping spaces reflect the fragmented subject, a mutilated society, a hollow culture, and at the same time they reflect themselves in a metaphor which, by the play of a mirror, reveals its own unreality. A whole reflection, which has been elaborated on the level of the *praxis* of the painters, takes as its starting-point the rectangular form of the picture and moves in the same direction. This rectangular character no longer appears, as it did in traditional painting, to be a natural, inoffensive notion; it is no longer a rule of common sense that is above suspicion. To contemplate the frame of a picture is already to interpret it as a constraint and to contest it. Jo Baer attacks the frame; in her use of the convention can be seen her denunciation of it, for she pushes it to an absurd extreme and causes a scandal by her excessive conformity—a "virgin," or whitened, canvas is framed with finicky deliberateness; the precision reveals her hate, for it exists without content; the frames are empty, like certain social frameworks. From Jo Baer to Pieter Engels the distance is less than one imagines; heavy hinged frames allow the canvas to be deformed and torn; the law of the frame asserts its own inconsistencies. The frame makes the picture into a show; it isolates it from its environment and offers it to the viewer as a thing apart. Engels reveals the ridiculous aspect of this show. Olitski on the other hand offers immense monochrome canvases (e.g. 11 ft. 5 in. $\times$ 21 ft. 6 in.); they are "vague" in color, or "dirty" from a traditional standpoint; a few brushstrokes and accidents on the extreme edge of the canvas create an image of a world at once mediocre and off-center; the purpose of these works seems to be

Christo (Javacheff), Bulgarian, 1935-
Corridor Store Front, 1966/1967
L. Braverman and Solo-Products Christo, New York

Josephine Baer, American, 1929-
Diptych, Verticals Flanking, 1967
Noah Goldowsky and Richard Bellamy, New York

Pieter Engels, Dutch, 1938-
Badly Constructed Canvas, 1967
Galerie 20; Amsterdam

to manifest their peculiar uselessness, and yet they are paradoxically fascinating. The viewer's eye is in some way drawn by the "blind" center of the canvas.

Our entire culture rests on the certainty of a universe in the fullness of completion, of man as a coherent, organized, and central being, and of a knowledge that is flawless. In a book on the events of May, Epistémon has pointed out the link between the French student uprising and the denunciation, as a hoax, of total knowledge;[6] fathers are no longer presumed to have knowledge. When the void appears, when negativity is not only conceived but put into action and exhibited, the established order finds itself contested. Doubtless Engels, Baer, and Christo only shake our sensibilities and not the world. This doesn't alter the fact that there has followed an undermining, a gradual destruction of what in the field of culture claimed to be full, perfect, and self-evident. There has been an assertion of the negative, which has entered the game like a trump card. To suggest and name non-being, assigning it a place in space, even metaphorically, is immediately to strike a blow at the Law of the Father. The logic of identity is questioned; non-being *is*; Parmenides' full, perfect sphere is shattered; each person is then shut out from himself. When Plato, in the *Sophist* (241 d), in order to define the simulacrum (*phantasma*), wishes "to prove that under a certain set of circumstances non-being exists and in some way being does not exist," he must kill Parmenides the Father—he claims to have achieved parricide.

The cold look

Linked with this theme of the void, the nihilist theme of the non-difference between values equally haunts contemporary art. Flaubert in his prophetic *Bouvard et Pécuchet* abolished hierarchies and differences with the same stroke: "Equality of everything, of good and evil, of the farcical and the sublime—of the Beautiful and the Ugly—of the insignificant and the characteristic. There are only facts, phenomena."[7] To state facts and tabulate them is an act of greater danger to society than righteous indignation. Whoever wants to judge bourgeois culture judges it in the name of a hierarchy of values which duplicates the social hierarchy and often justifies it. The *cold look* is more effective—it prepares the record and thus confronts what exists, revealing its scandalous or ridiculous aspects.

Bourgeois culture's attachment to old works of art is not allied only to the concept of heritage. To be sure, the bourgeoisie justifies its privileges by its knowledge of the past: "they can recognize mullion windows, late Gothic, and

68

early Renaissance. They are convinced that this fine knowledge justifies the preservation of their caste. They are intent on convincing the peasants of the necessity of safeguarding art, that is to say armchairs, that is to say the middle classes who know the best silk for covering a chair-back."[8] But old pictures are also an alibi for the bourgeoisie, allowing them to close their eyes to all that is modern. The established powers want art as pure amusement; they want either to forget the contemporary world or idealize it. The power of confrontation that exists in movies and which they often use in a very ambiguous manner[9] arises in part from the desire to describe the modern world, to utilize new techniques and materials and to unite art with science. They are at once a parody, exaltation, and mockery of industrial society; when the technical object becomes entertainment, it loses the purpose which defines it; it is a *perverted* mechanism. Traditional culture prefers that what it nourishes itself upon, what it protects and justifies, should not be exposed by the magnifying mirror of art. The cold look is too revealing a reflection of its oppressions, propaganda, and contradictions.

It's not by chance that Americans (Lichtenstein, Wesselmann, Andy Warhol, Rosenquist) are those above all who have triumphed when it comes to this reflection. Within the "American way of life" is a civilization that pushes to the *extreme* the successes and inevitable aberrations and pains of capitalism, and confronted by an unparalleled abundance of mass communications, they record what is imposed upon them and in that very way contest it. Their apparent passivity is both a fascination with the spectacle which is offered them and a revolt against it; they walk in the field that is strewn with society's mines so as to defuse them. After an Odyssey that takes them around the whole culture of their time, Bouvard and Pécuchet become wise; they copy. "No reflections! Let's copy! The page must be filled up, the monument completed";[10] they redouble and repeat this inanity and rejoice: "Joy at last!" Some American painters are the Bouvards and Pécuchets of the twentieth century—they copy posters and comic strips, imitating their style and technique. Sometimes, like Marcel Duchamp, their great forerunner, they sign manufactured objects, for example a can of Campbell's tomato soup. The image passes no judgment; it reveals the nightmare on the inside of paradise and the happy moments in hell. Wesselmann's nudes present the peculiarity of being both supersexed and desexualized, cold and obscene, repulsive and fascinating—women who display themselves so as to say no, who give themselves to be hated; their mouths are sexual organs and their nipples are pharmaceutical objects; they are the disquieting Penelopes of a strange Odyssey. No one will ever know who Lichtenstein's famous revolver is pointed at—at a capitalist or a revolutionary, a bandit or a policeman? It is simply there, threatening and ambiguous, a fantasy on the part of the spectator, which turns back against the spectator himself. Rosenquist uses the technique of the poster to evoke leisure and the countryside; he "participates" in a collective myth and at the same time coldly shuns it; he denounces society's utilization of this myth while simultaneously admiring this utilization and acknowledging his debt to it. "There are only facts, phenomena," said Flaubert. Traditional culture teaches prejudice, it insists that perception follow judgment; there are sights that must not be seen, or they must only be seen by those who have been *warned*. By a curious kind of Cartesianism the painter's *cold look* teaches us, on the contrary, to suspend our judgment, to discard all our old opinions and to rediscover behind the mask of values an experience necessarily ambiguous and terrifying; contrary to the Cartesian concept, everything is here accorded to perception. There is then the possibility of surprise, scandal, desire, and emotion. Free thought can emerge and explode the "take-it-for-granted" of an imposed ethic. "Now is the time to found institutes of deculture, schools of nihilism in which specially trained instructors would teach deconditioning and demystification..."[11] For too long, painting has been the instrument of moral didacticism, of the will to edify (*Erbauung*, as Hegel said in criticizing it); it has been used to elevate our thoughts and transmit a message. A negative didacticism is substituted for instruction in an assured knowledge of the self. Lack of knowledge can only shatter the illusion. The established order dislikes lucidity. It is high time that art make spectators into seers.

At the same time, the cold look constitutes a criticism of art itself. The artist is no longer a prophet or magus. Artistic production has been desanctified; it has voluntarily discarded its prestige and insisted repeatedly on this loss: it teaches us to become detached from it. It asserts its inferiority to the mere possibility of revolution.

Paean for the despicable

The confrontation of established values and the old hierarchy, and the rejection of hierarchy as such can take forms which, to a traditional way of thinking, are different from the technique of pure reportage. This movement eulogizes the despicable, depicts decay, and honors "dirty" materials, ineffectual gestures, and shameful spectacles; this reversal of the academic tradition is mistakenly seen by the upholders of that tradition as more radically violent than the simple refusal

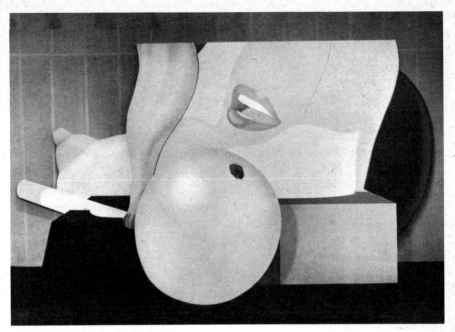

Tom Wesselmann, American, 1931-
Great American Nude No. 98, n.d.
Sidney Janis Gallery, New York

James Rosenquist, American, 1933-
Lanai, n.d.
John Powers, New York

to contrast the low with the high, the good with the bad, the beautiful with the ugly. Often the same revolutionary artists adopt successively or simultaneously the cold look and the paean for the despicable, the base, and the sordid. The two movements correspond to two different tactics; they are not fundamentally opposed. In this ideological guerilla war against the reigning culture (and perhaps against all culture), these two methods must be used in turn and, as often as possible, conjointly.

"I like to proclaim that my art is an enterprise to rehabilitate discredited values," wrote Jean Dubuffet in 1957.[12] In order to *deconstruct* established values, upset our habits of thought, undermine our concepts of man and the world in order to strike at the foundations of our culture, we must face aversions that we believe to be normal and natural; we must constantly criticize our idea of our own nature. In *Civilization and Its Discontents*, Freud advances the hypothesis that our civilization is linked to a suppression of the sense of smell, a profound disgust at strong odors; "it can be shown that the deepest root of sexual repression—a repression that parallels those of civilization—has its being in the organic defense mechanisms to which human nature had recourse at the stage of standing and walking upright with a view to preserving the mode of life established by this new position and preventing a return to the previous mode of animal existence." At this level, as at others, our present culture misuses certain prohibitions; the remotest allusion to our anality is considered reprehensible and nauseating. To wage war on our culture *also* means flouting this hidden norm and denouncing the repression that is all the more effective for being unspoken. This denunciation has been the aim of contemporary artists.

The steps they have taken are clarified in Georges Bataille's *The "old mole" and the prefix* sur *in the words* sur*homme and* sur*réaliste*.[13] Written before 1931 during an exchange with Breton, it reflected in the most accurate possible way an art that at that time was still to come. Bataille sees human life as "imprisoned and cocooned in its moral system." Only base materialism has the power to liberate us; he defines it as "recourse to all that is shocking, impossible to destroy, and even despicable, to all that debases and ridicules the spirit." Subversion is mistaken and lost when it *immediately* tries to create its own values and substitute them for those of the bourgeoisie. Bataille analyzes the metaphors of the eagle and the "old mole" that Marx speaks of. Revolution isn't a super-eagle (*suraigle*) in conflict with authoritarian imperialism and ascending into the radiant regions of sunniest heaven. It's an old mole that "digs holes in rotting soil that is repugnant to the delicate noses of the utopians"; among the idealists

Robert Rauschenberg, American, 1925-
Almanac 1962, 1962
Galerie Ileana Sonnabend, Paris

Yaacov Arman, Israeli, 1928-
Big Horn Creek, 1967
Sidney Janis Gallery, New York

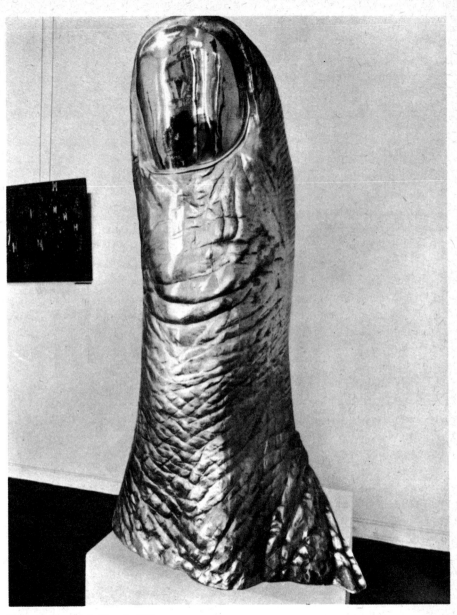

César (Baldacchini), French, 1921-
Pouce, n.d.

we find that devaluation of smell that was observed by Freud. Bataille questions the concept of beauty and all "elevated" ideas. He quotes Marx for whom "in history as in nature, decay is the laboratory of life." The passage ends with a sentence both confident and terrified: "It's by digging the stinking ditch of bourgeois culture that we shall perhaps see opening in the depths of the subsoil the immense and sinister caves where human strength and liberty will establish themselves in the shelter of all those orders of a God who today commands the most idiotic elevation of the spirit of each and every man."

Of course, artistic production isn't revolution in itself; to identify it with the *old mole* would be idealistic prejudice; but it can undermine and degrade and hence become its ally.

From this point of view, the artist's main task is performed at the level of *matter*. Jean Dubuffet in his at times impassioned rehabilitation of matter, attacks an Aristotelianism which, whether consciously or not, survives in us. Matter is no longer a subordinate; it has been given a chance to "resist"; "one must give full rein to all the dangers that are inherent in the material used";[14] "I also love the embryonic, the malformed, the imperfect, the composite."[15] At the same time the distinction between beautiful, noble, durable materials and vile, scorned, fragile materials is abolished. *The little statues of precarious life* (1954) were made of Jex tampons, crumpled newspapers, unsalable sponges and various rubbish, thus ridiculing the use of marble and bronze. The materials that culture considers ignoble and repugnant have, according to Dubuffet, the most power to move us: "In the Sahara, when the Arabs have something to putty or a hole to stop up, they use a paste that they make by kneading dates with goat's dung and a little sand. That's a mixture that excites me a great deal, and I certainly hope to use it one day."[16]

At least since Schwitters' astonishing collages, *Merz* (c. 1920), art has never ceased to be interested in scraps and rubbish; our society is revealed by its droppings. Beside surfaces that are sometimes painted in an almost classic manner, Rauschenberg places on the canvas some "dirty" scrawls, some finger marks, some stains; he glues to the canvas an old rotting plank, a shabby stuffed bird, or a dusty rag; the moldy, the fetid, and the rusty take on an extraordinary splendor in his works. Those of Jasper Johns tend in the same direction. Tinguely's useless, complex machines are composed of elements that are worn out, outdated, and inadequate for the function the artist imposes on them; they are parodies and mockeries of the industrial world, and their aim is to come apart and collapse in abrupt, clumsy movements. In today's art, the dirty is extolled

76

and the sordid exalted. In western culture, cleanliness and propriety are linked. The present confrontation denies both simultaneously. It befouls (at least for the moment) its own nest; it defiles the walls; it exposes to a culture that doesn't want to see them the existence of decay and death.

The subject matter itself doesn't avoid putrefaction and scatology. Art reflects a *corrupt* world. Objects melt and flow like the monsters described by Lovecraft. Faces become blurred and bodies decompose; so it is with Bacon. With odds and ends the American artist Thek creates scenes of putrefaction, the image of a rotting world. Some of César's gigantic "expansions" can evoke nothing except an excreted reality; psychoanalysts have stressed the link between what man *makes* and his feces, and the provocative objects that César has created reveal this link.

Thus the painter's status is called into question. The properties of an honest, painstaking, meticulous work of art no longer interest him. He dislikes the idea that he may seem an ideal artisan or a conscientious demiurge. He doesn't want to contribute to this hoax. Arman makes a work of art out of crushed tubes and squirting colors—the material of the traditional picture becomes the creation itself. César offers a series of thumbprints—the shaping agent of traditional sculpture pays itself mocking homage: monuments that owe their shape to the sculptor's thumb affirm the uselessness of such "paw-strokes." The old concept of the creative gesture is contested in the works themselves; the new relations between the artistic producer and his product are not yet defined.

The omnipresence of eroticism

As in Georges Bataille's manifesto, *The history of the eye*, eroticism emerges as something scandalous at the outset of this defense of the despicable; and while distinct from this defense, it is at the same time linked to the assertion of it. It is ceasing to shy away from scrutiny, to mask itself, and to disguise its power. Desire offers itself as a spectacle in all its complexities and perversions. The obstacles that are encountered in representing it arise from its own contradictions, not from social prohibitions. Art is ceasing to be an alibi for morals; it no longer wants to "sublimate" the gestures of love or to disguise the sexual organs; it is not opposed to "healthy and normal" love or an eroticism considered morbid by respectable people.

It is clear that the fight against sexual repression is not, as some imagine, the essence of the revolutionary struggle. It is equally probable, as Freud points out in opposition to Reich, that a good society is not equal to ensuring perfect enjoyment that is fully accessible and free from danger for those who experience it. All the same the attack on our culture, which has been excessively repressive in this respect according to Freud himself, demands an examination of our taboos, particularly those that prevent us from appreciating our bodies and accepting without shame our own desire and that of others. In May 1968, a wall inscription proclaimed, "I rejoice in the paving-stones." Another was more precise: "The more I make revolution, the more I want to make love; the more I make love, the more I want to make revolution." These slogans affirm the need to unite the struggle against police repression with the liberation of our own desires. Contemporary artists are dedicating their greatest efforts to this fight for enjoyment.

In the eyes of rigid moralists the exhibition *Documenta 4* could have seemed a veritable sexual pandemonium. The reviews of exhibitions more and more resemble medieval descriptions of a witches' sabbat. Hockney's homosexual fantasies invade his pictures quite openly, or with a minimum of disguise. Allen Jones expresses foot fetishism and suggests the closeness between the art object and the fetish. The Frenchman Malaval isolates a woman's legs and "focalizes" her knees and pubes; only the erogenous zones on which the painter's and the viewer's desire centers can be properly seen; the rest of the body is an abstract diagram; the woman's piecemeal body becomes a trap for men. In a willfully naive style, Richard Lindner depicts enormous women from a masochistic dream. Obscene puppets spread their legs amidst old-fashioned bourgeois furniture, facing a photograph of General MacArthur; one, with her throat pierced by a rose, lies on a sewing-machine. In this salacious, antiquated setting (so perfect for a Klossowski novel) spectators sit on armchairs and sofas, where they are uneasy strangers to one another; the eroticism suggested by the American Kienholz neither unites individuals nor reassures them; it isolates them, distresses them, and renders them incomprehensible to one another. A cast by George Segal shows a woman spectator contemplating with an air of indifference a copulation that is congealed, conclusively interrupted, immobilized, eternalized. With its mirrors on the ceiling and floor, Megert's room is a voyeur's paradise and hell—he sees, but never enough, or for long enough; the painted work, the sublimation of voyeurism, is replaced by an "environment" in which the voyeur can pass on to the act, to the interior of space multiplied to infinity.

The unmasked presence of sexuality emerges in places where it is least expected. The imprints of female bodies on a canvas by Yves Klein show traces of the absent

Allen Jones, English, 1937-
Number 1: What do You Mean? What do You Mean?, 1968
Tooth Gallery, London

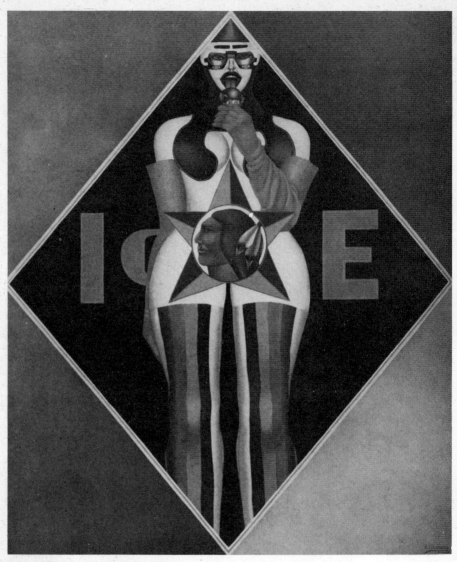

Richard Lindner, American, 1901-
  Ice, 1966
  Whitney Museum of American Art, New York

Edward Kienholz, American, 1927-
Roxy's, 1960/1961
Dwan Gallery, New York

81

she, the sign of a lack that summons desire. Manders' white geometry brings the viewer a vanishing image, a deceptive evocation of a breast or a pair of buttocks, the semblance of a penetration.

Jean Dubuffet is rightly concerned that the artist may employ erotic images to the point of abusing them: "Dismiss breasts and buttocks... Nowadays these erotic themes in art are so overdone that it is in avoiding them that art can still scandalize."[17] However, in this very field of eroticism, Dubuffet is the great liberator. The extraordinary graffiti illustrating *Labonfam Abeber* (1950) are an irreplaceable repertoire of amorous gestures;[18] the freedom of the bodies is expressed in spontaneous draughtsmanship; this liberty is preliminary to all *true* liberation. In *Women's Bodies* there is no exaggerated respect for the female body. It is delivered and displayed; as in certain primitive paintings, the sex is indicated by emphatic strokes; "all feeling for decency is violated."[19] In "a sort of continuous, universal soup with the taste of life about it,"[20] the human is not distinguished from the inhuman—flesh is mingled with textures that suggest soils and rinds and instill our bodies with strange and manifest desires. The loved object is endangered; but "it is when things are in extreme danger that their excellence begins to sing";[21] one can't separate the enjoyment of the risks enjoyment brings from the final danger of death. A false veneration of the female body, its idealization, originated in that Greek art which Dubuffet does not admire. Dubuffet on the other hand loves and desires woman; while employing certain excesses and a deliberate obscenity, he depicts her without falsifying her. She disquiets and fascinates as she is revealed to herself and others. She is painted in the way she is desired and, perhaps, in the way she sees herself, in the way she lives her desire for pleasure and experiences her body.

Writing and figuration

Indiana's game with the four letters of the word *Love* takes us from the realm of eroticism to that of writing. We shall consider its theoretical limits and only pause to observe certain landmarks in this style. The study of the relation between the practice of writing, the way this practice is reflected, and the act of confrontation is a task for scientific inquiry. It is significant that writing, the formation of letters, has been analyzed with particular thoroughness in the last years; its theoreticians have enabled our age to relate the sickness it is undergoing, the crisis that presses upon it, and the phenomenon of writing.

George Segal, American, 1924-
Legend of Lot, 1966
Sidney Janis Gallery, New York

Christian Megert, Swiss, 1936-
   Miroir,1961/1968

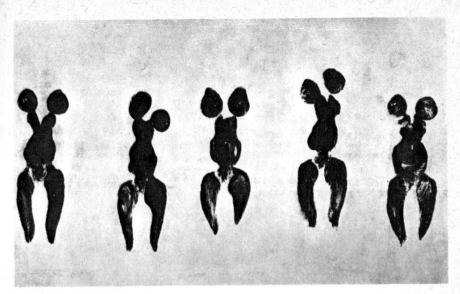

Yves Klein, French, 1928-1962
Anthropometrie No. 82, 1960
Musée des Arts Décoratifs, Paris

Jos Manders, Dutch, 1934-
Communication, 1967

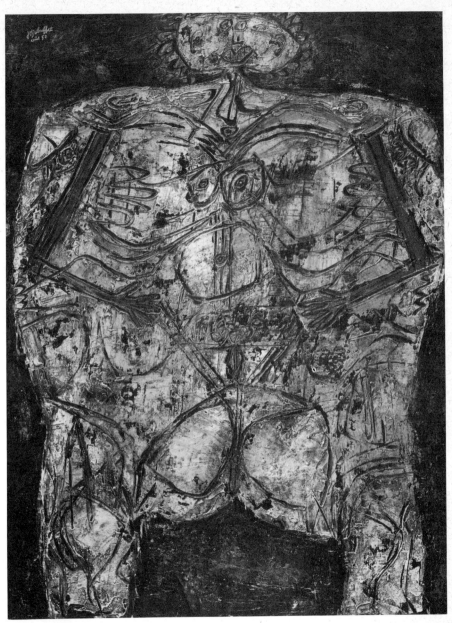

Jean Dubuffet, French, 1901-
Corps de femme paysagé, 1950

Though this is still difficult to conceptualize, we have an inkling of the way in which writing is linked with desire, pleasure, violence, death, and absence.[22] We do not know how writing and subversion are connected; we can, however, affirm the importance of wall-newspapers in the Chinese cultural revolution, and of the mural inscriptions during the uprising of May 1968. It is not enough to write in order to be revolutionary, even if one writes like Lenin; but writing cannot be an inoffensive act when it is against the established order. The act of writing is a transgression against the law that is already made, against the book already written.

Now, one of the characteristics of contemporary art consists in violently introducing the letter into painting. The cubist example and the calligraphic tradition do not sufficiently explain the frequency of this procedure. The influence of Magritte, although more important than people imagine, is only occasional. A curious tendency is subverting the traditional differences between figuration and the naming of things. The letter is presented as an image; the form may be replaced by the name, for the name in some way lends power to the viewer's imagination. We have cited Indiana's work. Jasper Johns and Dine also play with letters and numbers. In his *Signs*, the Czech artist Kolár swathes objects in musical notation, manuscripts, and Hebrew letters; he deprives these objects of their nature, introducing the distance of writing between an apple or a spoon and the viewer. Arakawa goes even further; with or without humor he replaces the normally represented form by the name of that form; the picture surface indicates the reciprocal relationship of the objects—the chair is under the mirror, above the window. Fetishism is partly conjured up; the esthetic attitude becomes difficult; the thing is defined by its name and place.

Environments

Creating environments is another means the artist has of attacking the art of the past. This often complements previous attacks. We have already seen examples—the empty, closed rooms of Christo are images of the void; Megert's glass room and Kienholz's living room are special abodes of eroticism. Kinetic rooms allow us to enter a universe of festivity—an air of playfulness is created, and there is the possibility of another order from the one that is usually imposed; society accepts a kind of disorder, but one that is limited by the confines of the room and the rules of "propriety." One may be spontaneous, under the

88

Robert Indiana, American, 1928-
  Love, 1967 (serigraph)
  Galerie der Spiegel, Cologne

Jiři Kolář, Czech, 1914-
  Homage to Christian Morgenstern, 1965/1966

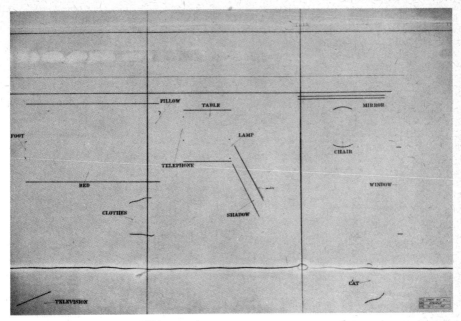

Shusaka Arakawa, Japanese, 1936-
Alphabet Skin No. 3, 1966/1967
Dwan Gallery, New York

surveillance of guardians.   There is no longer a separation between the work and the spectator, who can change it and become its co-author; but he changes it without running any risks and without any great possibilities for modification. He has the right to walk, sit, look, and press one or two buttons.   His liberty is programmed and usually reduced to a puerile illusion.   The free act becomes too facile—at the moment when the viewer is invited to manipulate the object, he is in fact himself manipulated by it.

If the festivities created by environments involve waste and expense, they do so in an inoffensive way, for neither society nor the viewer nor the work itself runs the least danger.   They anticipate death and are an image of it, but we are forewarned that "it's only for laughs."   The free act ceases to be a rare act, a difficult act, an act involving commitment, an effective act whose effect is often irreversible. A spurious liberty coincides with an imaginary death—we are at the opposite pole from revolutionary festivity.

Nevertheless, environments fascinate us and transform us.   They possess a power of negation.   They obligate us to use our bodies and to accept the idea of seeing them reflected.   They encourage in us a spontaneity that enables us to escape from what Moreno calls "canned culture."   They bring out the absurdity of those rectangles hung on the wall by a nail, to revert to Dubuffet's definition[23] of pictures.   They tend to reduce our passivity, to bridge the gap between us and the work, and to bring us closer to the other viewers.   However imperfect and deceptive these environments may be, they remain the image of the myth that is dreamed by the rebellious and the unsubdued: "There will be no more onlookers in my city—nothing but actors.   No more culture and hence no more looking. No more theater—theater comes with the division into stage and auditorium. In my city everyone will be on the stage."[24]   It is of little importance whether this myth is realizable or not.   It lies on the horizon of our rejection.   "Don't worry about what will be at the end of the road.   Roads have no ends, no ends that are attainable."[25]

Ambiguities of artistic confrontation

Thus contemporary art finds itself in a peculiar situation.   It attacks culture, inside which it has arisen.   It criticizes society and reverses the scale of values or denies the existence of one; it recommends unflagging confrontation.   "Art's true mission is subversive, its true nature is such that it would make sense to ban it

92

and harass it."[26] It challenges itself. Everything is transformed before our eyes—the conception of the artist's job, the position of the viewer, the form of works of art, their value, and their materiality. At every moment, though often in a confused way, art marks the limits of its revolutionary power. It is allied to the "old mole," but couldn't replace it. Neither theories nor works of art will shake the world. Art gives rise to works whose sole force lies in their unceasing *denial*. Today every true artist can say with Mallarmé, "Destruction was my Beatrice."

Faced with this negativity which doesn't spare even itself, society is put on the defensive. Bourgeois culture has a limitless fund of tricks—it shuts up works of art in museums and salons, and turns spectators away from them; it mocks and scorns new ways of seeing, doing, and thinking; it buys and sells works of art and justifies their economic value by their esthetic value and vice versa; it utilizes whatever attacks it in order to prove its liberalism; it diffuses it in order to diminish the power of the scandal; it keeps it for an "elite"; it loses it in a vast, imaginary museum.

But these tricks are not always completely effective. The confrontation continues—and the undermining. Values waver; certainties are split asunder. We desire an unforeseeable future, but one that will break entirely with existing norms. Our reason and our whimsy coincide to bring it about. This future, as Derrida wrote, "can only be announced and presented in the form of a monstrosity."[27]

1. Rosa LUXEMBURG, quoted in the journal *Le Pavé*, May, 1968.
2. The importance of geographic and geological metaphors in contemporary thought has been well noted by M. Foucault.
3. H. MICHAUX, *Ecuador*, NRF, p. 93.
4. *Op. cit.*, p. 99.
5. *Documenta 4*, Kassel, Germany, June 27-October 6, 1968. All the illustrations to this essay, with the exception of the Arman and the Dubuffet, are of works included in *Documenta 4* at Kassel and have been reproduced from the catalog of that great exhibition.
6. EPISTÉMON, *Ces idées qui ont ébranlé la France*, Fayard, pp. 19-21.
7. *Bouvard et Pécuchet*, Vol. II, Denoël, 1966, pp. 52-53.
8. J. DUBUFFET, *Asphyxiante culture*, Pauvert, p. 10.
9. Cf. G. LASCAULT, "La fête cinétique," *Temps modernes*, November, 1967.
10. FLAUBERT, *Bouvard et Pécuchet*, Livre de Poche, p. 447.
11. J. DUBUFFET, *Asphyxiante culture*, p. 151.
12. J. DUBUFFET, *Prospectus et tous écrits suivants*, Vol. II, p. 135.
13. Published and presented by Denis HOLLIE in *Tel Quel*, No. 34, pp. 5-17.
14. J. DUBUFFET, *Prospectus et tous écrits suivants*, Vol. I, p. 59.

15. *Op. cit.*, Vol. I, p. 88.

16. *Op. cit.*, Vol. I, p. 466.

17. *Op. cit.*, Vol. I, p. 80.

18. *Catalogue des travaux de J. Dubuffet*, Pauvert, Section V, p. 83-90.

19. J. DUBUFFET, *Prospectus et…*, Vol. II, p. 74.

20. *Op. cit.*, Vol. II, p. 119.

21. *Op. cit.*, Vol. II, p. 73.

22. DERRIDA, *De la grammatologie*, Éditions de Minuit,, *L'écriture et la différence*, Seuil, J.F. LYOTARD, "Le travail du rêve ne pense pas," *Revue d'Esthétique*, January-March 1968, pp.26-61. S. LECLAIRE, *Psychanalyser*, Seuil, explores the link between enjoyment and the letter. See also the entire works of Maurice Blanchot.

23. J. DUBUFFET, *Asphyxiante culture*, p. 100.

24. *Op. cit.*, p. 116.

25. *Op. cit.*, p. 118.

26. J. DUBUFFET, *Prospectus et tous écrits suivants*, Vol. II, p. 322.

27. DERRIDA, *De la grammatologie*, p. 14.

Gérald Gassiot-Talabot

Is confrontation possible?

The young painter Quintanilla, a Peruvian Indian who returns in his work to the elements of a fantastic bestiary, told me that he had stopped painting revolutionary pictures, in spite of his desire to do so, as a result of a misadventure that remained with him as a painful memory. Seeing every day scenes of brutality and exploitation, he painted a large-scale picture of a landowner with a furious glint in his eye, whipping from astride his horse a throng of panic-stricken peasants. He then took it to a gallery in Lima. Imagine his surprise when it was bought shortly afterward by one of the richest "exploiters" in the country, a prize ruffian who exclaimed (without the least trace of black humor), "There's a picture that shows how Indians should be treated!"

This type of ambiguity in immediate meaning is one of the crudest and commonest difficulties one can raise concerning revolutionary painting. The least one can say is such painting goes through a hell paved with good intentions and that the worst often prevails over the best. That is all the more reason to examine the limits and possibilities of this political and moral attitude toward the world and the choices it entails for the painter.

The *raison d'être*, the methods of expression and development, and even the content of revolutionary art come up against obstacles and queries of such importance that it would be futile to try to disguise them.

In the summer of 1967 I organized an exhibition called "The World in Question" at the Museum of Modern Art of the City of Paris within the framework of ARC.[1] In writing the preface to the catalog, I pondered the existence of those revolutionary painters whom Pierre Gaudibert and I chose to include by showing a few of their representative works: "Isn't the very nature of art to rebel against the decay and stiffening of forms and to search for new modes of vision at the price of brutal rejection and periodic questioning?" In this perspective, are not the march of art and the negations it gives rise to righted by the most effective confrontation, the only acceptable kind for the painter and the sculptor? Those who oppose painting that is concerned with content (and they include the champions of constructivist and kinetic art) call upon the artist to innovate by distortion. And it needs all the conviction and experience of an Alain Jouffroy to write, "We know from the example of Havana that art for the sake of revolution is a revolution in art"; nor is this assertion a frivolous play on words, as some would claim. It means that we must adopt other criteria than those that have normally prevailed in western society since the time of Impressionism, if we wish, after the frightful blunder of socialist realism, to give an unbiased welcome to those painters who have decided to find the way back to a political art.

We have thus reached that moment of agonizing reappraisal when in a world that is cracking and splitting on every side, art can no longer exist as an autonomous area from which forms can expand as if by osmosis to fertilize and mold other sectors of human existence. The majority of those who have concerned themselves with contemporary ideas are agreed in assigning a new vocation to the heritage of forms, but their primary concern is to integrate the artist into the system by giving him the role of a great organizer of sensibility, an engineer of vision. As an extreme measure they contemplate new means of distribution that will bypass the dealer, the closed system of promotion and sale; they advocate multiples, the enlargement of the market, a struggle to control speculation, etc. If these courses of action are necessary components, we must still realize that the vehicle of forms remains a powerful emotional, demonstrative, and critical agent and that the artist who wants to make his convictions and his art coincide tries to use the latter as a weapon. There remains the problem of discovering if this weapon is an artistic act and reciprocally, if this act is an effective weapon.

We should do well to recognize that it is often impossible to reply in the affirmative to the two complementary terms of this proposition. We frequently come across pictures that purport to be works of confrontation and yet have not managed to adapt their means to their ends; laboriously they use utterly bankrupt methods, so that they lack necessity and conviction. From this point, it is only a short step to the claim that *all* revolutionary painting suffers from this failing, that political involvement is one thing and artistic creation another, that those artists who try to express content use that and their disarmingly good

96

Group of artists painting a mural
dedicated to the Cuban revolution,
Havana, 1967.

A painting by Bernard Rancillac
at the May 1967
exhibition in Havana.

intentions as a cover for the poverty of their artistic invention. This kind of attack was seen to develop at the very heart of the events in May 1968, even on the platform of the Institute of Art and Archaeology; here the young painters' Salon, whose directors were all in the fighting, contributed to the state of mind of one art critic who came close to hysteria. These very excesses show to what extent this subject awakens in each of us profound reactions that are based on the fear that an artistic dictatorship of the Stalinist type may return, on the anxious concern at discovering in a painting the opportunism and imposture that is sometimes only a mode among other modes.

We must, however, before going further, emphasize that there is no incompatibility between the search for a language of expression and the search for content. On the contrary, it is in the impulse of political choice, in the search for particularly bitter and inflammatory subjects, that many artists have found the motivation necessary to remain at the height of their inspiration and aims without becoming facile or complaisant. It would seem that by an inescapable process the importance of the subject releases new possibilities in the rendering. Besides, the dramatic impact of an unspeakable deed can be as powerful a stimulant as exaltation at a happy allegiance. Thus it was that in the case of Rancillac a bitter, grating work like "Enfin! Silhouette affinée jusqu'à la taille" has as much impact as the figure of Castro that was painted in the sweltering Cuban summer for the museum in Havana. This shows we must never lose sight of the frontier that divides denunciation (torture in Vietnam) from adherence to an ideal, even if voluntary (e.g. homage to Fidel Castro), socialist realism having for the most part produced only painting of enforced praise. In any case, the problems posed by Rancillac in his series of topical pictures go beyond anecdote; the time of day is objectively indicated (by clocks in the three views of Cuba at morning, midday, and evening), but above all it is the contemplation of the power of the image, of the separation of this image from its iconographic reproduction (the image of the image) that serves as a Trojan Horse to subversive thought. To meaning founded on problems of space, which has been handled by Pop Art with extreme thematic ambiguity, European "narrative" painting has added a grasp of history. This history, however, is not seen in a flat or discursive relationship but with brutal and arresting concern; the unification in time of different moments, the shock of key images, the significant treatment of texture (Spadari's downy surface, Monory's breaks in plane, Sarkis' optical gearing down, Alleyn's schematization, the "video" effect of value equivalences practiced by Rancillac, etc.) unite in forming a cluster of symbols,

Bernard Rancillac, French, 1932-
Enfin! Silhouette affinée jusqu'à la taille, 1967. Galerie B. Mommaton, Paris

a synthesis in which the narrative process and the representation tend to become submerged beneath the total situation of powerful shock.

However, it is pointless to go on with the enumeration of the particular stylistic tendencies of the main painters in "The World in Question," for the problem does not lie in the forms that many artists give us as a kind of supplement. Besides, it is as a "supplement" that certain painters who make a point of the peculiarities in their treatment achieve that thing we call *cachet*—a flavor or a specific irony. So it is with the pictures of Arroyo, Erro, Recalcati, Biras, Cuéco, Tisserant, or Parré.

There is nothing surprising in the fact that this list should include some of the leading spirits behind the young painters' Salon, which in the last years has put on view the new generations of artists in France and abroad. It was this salon which in 1965 and 1966, in an objective certified report, assembled all that was to be reverenced in Paris in the years following, and in 1967 turned in the direction of austere design and restricted its choice to a requirement that went contrary to the prevailing formalism. For its intention to be "at once objective and partisan instead of being eclectic and liberal" (a formula that met with some success in 1966), it substituted the next year an intransigence that provoked some gnashing of teeth. If we refer to the indroductory essay in the 1967 catalog we find a truly revolutionary code that is unique to this organization, nor does its originality bear the readily recognizable stamp of Gilles Aillaud. The young painters' Salon defined its action as follows: "This action aims at liberating art from the shackles imposed by estheticism, which is holding it as a prisoner within the indeterminate domain of cultural concepts; art must, on the contrary, be placed in direct relation to life and history"; and with an allusion to the "objectivity" of the previous salon, the essay continues: "One may say that the systematic opening up of new stylistic possibilities has perhaps caused some changes in taste as to forms, but it has done nothing to reawaken the spirit. In fact, beneath the deceptive freedom of manner, what is vital in a picture today is completely camouflaged, hidden in the adherence of the picture to an 'option,' that is to say one of the categories, one of the departments whereby the more and more oppressive reign of esthetic analysis administers the world of the arts.

"The threat behind this generalized formalism is an immense dream of integration, of participation in the life of modern bourgeois technical society. We are witnessing the exploitation of vital energies by culture, whose sole ambition is to keep in step with the intoxicating novelties of science and industry.

"Hence, we must not be surprised if the same reasons that prompted the

Giangiacomo Spadari, Italian,
Per un potere operaio, III, 1968
Galleria Bergamini, Milan

Erro (Gundmundur Gundmundsson), Icelandic, 1932-
Pierrot, 1964
Galleria Schwarz, Milan

Erro (Gundmundur Gundmundsson), Icelandic, 1932-
  The Bay of Pigs, 1967
  Museum of Modern Art, Havana

Eduardo Arroyo, Spanish, 1937-
Spana te Miro, 1967
Galleria Marconi, Milan

committee to fight the traditional rhetoric of the language of forms compel them today to fight on several other fronts, for example against the proliferation of found objects and in general against all that plays on the nerves and thus tends to anesthetize the sensibility rather than stimulate the activity of the spirit.

"Contrary to what we are urged to believe, true liberty is very far away. However limited the power of art may be today, it must be put in the service of this truth."

If we ponder these words and decide that the intentions they contain should be applied with the utmost possible rigor, we can't help noting the impressive attempt to give confrontation a collective form. However, as this confrontation covered a wide gamut in the visual arts and as the directors of the salon were loath to give precise directives, we were faced, in the very midst of this manifestation, with an attempt at concerted action within the most clear-cut limits. This was the "red," or "Vietnamese," room which gathered twenty-five painters around the theme, "The war waged by the Vietnamese people against American imperialism," the genesis and realization of which have been described by Michel Troche.[2] It is interesting to note, as he has himself revealed, what kind of difficulties immediately beset this initiative. Once the theme had been chosen, the technical matters had been straightened out, and the framework of the debate had been determined, "there remained the problem of defining the manner in which the chosen content should be treated. But how can one here divide the 'manner' from the objective decided upon? To paint the war in Vietnam was not simply to illustrate a news item or give an esthetic description of an object; it was to get inside an essential situation which in its human and social aspects imposed a mode of vision and expression." Each exhibitor had to conform to a necessary legibility without being forced to change his language of expression, hence the undertaking was a collective one in which preliminary sketches were discussed and modified in response to the opinion of the group. While bringing into question the principle of the "artistic personality," this method preserved a character of spontaneity, enthusiasm, and liberty which was far removed from the vexatious bureaucratic practices of the defunct socialist realism.

This Vietnamese room could not be seen by the public because the 1968 salon was postponed on account of the events of May, but the aspiration toward a collective art, which is found in other sectors of the art world (le Groupe de Recherche d'Art Visuel) but which is most frequently and thoroughly practiced by revolutionary painters, remains. Arroyo, Aillaud, and Recalcati had already joined together to paint "Live and let die, or the murder of Marcel Duchamp." The deliberately anonymous, uniform treatment created just as much of a scandal as the violation of a taboo by the picture's theme.   In Spain, the groups Cronica and Realidad have for some years been carrying on a struggle which is not in the least platonic, while all the painters who were in Cuba during July 1967 remember the atmosphere of public gaiety and collective exaltation in which the Havana mural was created.   It was dedicated to the Cuban Revolution and was the work of several dozen artists and writers of all nationalities.

We have just seen how the search for a clear, precise, definite treatment could lead certain artists to abolish style and seek a provocative banality of effect that was destined to *reduce the subject to itself* in the same way as others brought back the object to its reality as an object, or as Buren, Mosset, Toroni, and others offered identical canvases that were only what they were.   The radical action on the part of Arroyo, Aillaud, and Recalcati did not constitute a return to the academicism of post-office calendars, for that would have been ridiculous, but a radical rejection of any mediation by sensibility, expression, or originality of form with a view to making a clear, significant statement.   At the extremity that is equivalent to the constructivist or lyric *tabula rasa* of abstraction, and in the context of the sophisticated estheticism of western art, it is clear that such a choice can lay claim to all the criteria of non-art.

The search for legibility that we were speaking about is linked with the desire for effectiveness that is imperative in a period of crisis such as the one we are living in.   I find it intriguing that a certain critic, whose reactionary sentiments are notorious, should recognize, after having tried to hook his little problems onto the movement of May 1968, that "modern painting and revolutionary action don't marry well except in the street and on walls."   One of the aims of revolutionary art is to be on walls in the form of posters, for at the moment of political and social convulsion it is there that the painters who have been bent on determined action find "full employment."   We must remember that if the popular studio at the Beaux-Arts took so effective a part in the struggle of May 1968, working for action committees and strikers, it is not only because of the unity achieved among painters of different tendencies, but also because among the most resolute minds there were artists who gave themselves to figurative work and pictorial confrontation.

These observations must not obscure the fact that the revolutionary field has its limits.   It is abundantly clear, in fact, that revolutionary art is difficult to define; it suffers from so many ambiguities, and it runs the risk of being stifled

Groupe Cronica
La Cantidao se transforma en Calidao, 1966

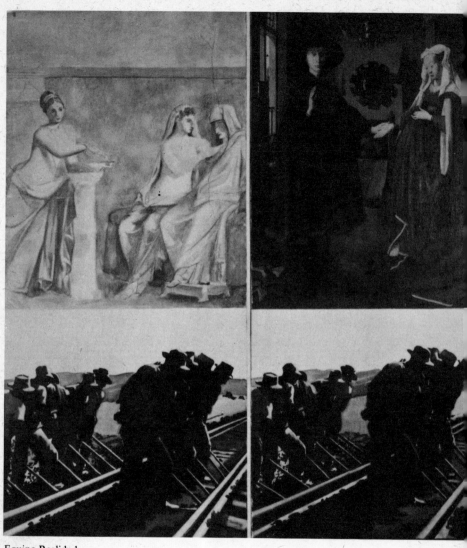

Equipo Realidad
«*C'était une fois...*», 1965/1966

Edgard Naccache, Tunisian, 1924-
Peinture, 1968

by so many awkward good intentions; it asserts convictions, choices, and a conception of the artist's role in the community that many do not share. Not only must there be a non-revolutionary art, but we must recognize that many of the works that are of contemporary significance for us have nothing to do with political action. All authoritarianism on this score would involve the danger of Jdanovism and interfere with the natural leanings of those creative temperaments that have nothing to do with this field on account of esthetic choices that are irreconcilable with it. A revolutionary impulse, no matter how many modern artists have opened the way, from Picasso to Matta and the Mexican fresco painters, is a matter of generation and must be understood as such. On the other hand, if we recognize that political involvement is often independent of the pictorial manner that is practiced, we shall appreciate the Cuban government's policy of an open artistic pluralism. Cuban artists choose political themes only if and when they want to; moreover the manner of treating these themes is not subject to any censorship. For example, the exhibition *Painters and guerillas*, of 1967, comprised weapons, photographic documents, and pictures in the widest imaginable range of styles. I am not saying that the result was in every way satisfactory, but the field of action that such freedom can develop allows evolutionary mechanisms to function normally, and that is the essential. There is a temperament that considers art a means of combat, a vehicle for ideas, a militant witness, and an involvement. I don't think it was the desire to flatter the western artists who gathered in Havana for the May Exhibition that prompted the head of the Vietnamese delegation to say that a picture was worth as much as a grenade or a rifle. The few words he spoke in the course of that meeting could have served as a preface—and what a preface!—to the exhibition "The World in Question," which had been ridiculed in France by some of the thoughtful left-wingers.

In this action, the combat zones and the available means are plentiful. All the artists are engaged, for even if the problems of content concern only some of them, many are aroused by other aspects of subversion; among these are the bypassing of the market through multiples, collective creative work, manifestations organized in the street for a public that is not prepared for the diffusion of culture (by the GRAV, for instance), criticism of the consumer society, and dramatization by pictorial means that are close to abstraction (Hernandez, Millares), figurative expressionism (Lora, Ortega), Surrealism (Camacho) etc.

The very mutiplicity of the points of impact and ways of intervention increase the possibilities of misunderstanding. The ambiguity as to meaning, for example,

111

Roberto Matta (Echaurren), Chilean, 1912-
La Chasse aux Adolescents: Aveugler, Faire Pleurer, 1968
Galerie Alexandre Iolas, Paris

which we mentioned at the beginning with reference to Quintanilla, is inherent in very nature of the act of painting, which is rarely univocal, even when the main meaning is clearly defined. This ambiguity can obtain as to style (Fautrier's *Hostages* and Lapoujade's *Riots*), to the sign constituted by such and such a form (the sense of crowd in Genoves), to simple legibility (Monory's painting entitled *After the rain*, which gave rise to various interpretations in Cuba), to different degrees of meaning that are implanted by the painter like explosive relays, or stages, to the verge of indescribability, to the *a posteriori* meaning that the artist or the public sometimes finds in a work of art.

Thus the historico-political implications of the very lovely canvas that Télémaque had painted for the exhibition *Narrative figuration in contemporary art* (Galerie Creuze, 1965), the subject of which seemed to be the American intervention in Santo Domingo, were minimized by the artist in the course of later discussions; and it was impossible to determine if a mistake had been made from the start as to the picture's content or if its meaning had evolved with the painter's esthetic concepts.

What other difficulties are there besides this ambiguity of meaning? Isn't there a contradiction, for example, between effectiveness and visual pleasure? Mustn't the revolutionary artist beware of the traps of "manner," of a facile hand or imagination, of the non-adaptation of style to subject, of mechanical complications and visual gadgets that distract the attention, of the insidious interference of mental activity in the objective field of the picture? The last point brings us back to ambiguity of meaning, for if a Monory deliberately suggests a multiplicity of solutions (*Comme il vous plaira*) and plays on the interference of his subjectivity with the real image, if someone like Klasen doesn't dissociate the object from experience of the object, how many other artists, less lucid, are no longer even aware that all they are doing is delineating things in detail while believing that they are sacrificing themselves to noble ambitions and serving a cause?

Ultimately it is the contradiction between form and content that lies at the very heart of every artistic measure that attempts to establish a unity between these antagonisms. On the other hand, the evolution of contemporary esthetic concepts and, one must add, the secondary influence of Pop Art on all western art have brought about an approximate idea of what constitutes "artistic quality." We have recently seen it in the case of art in the street. How is one to react, for example, to this extract from Mao Tse-tung's little red book which to a hasty reader might seem a condemnation of all explicit art (the style of the slogan

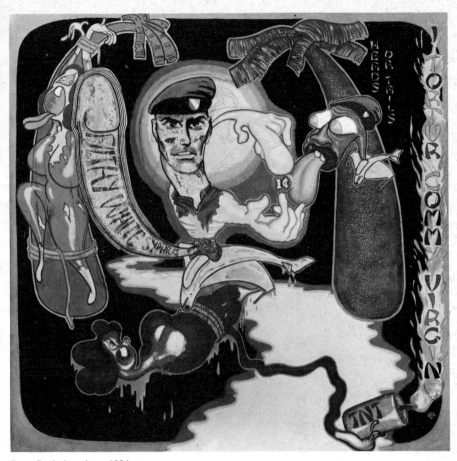

Peter Saul, American, 1934-
  I Torture Commy Virgins, 1967
  Galerie Darthea Speyer, Paris

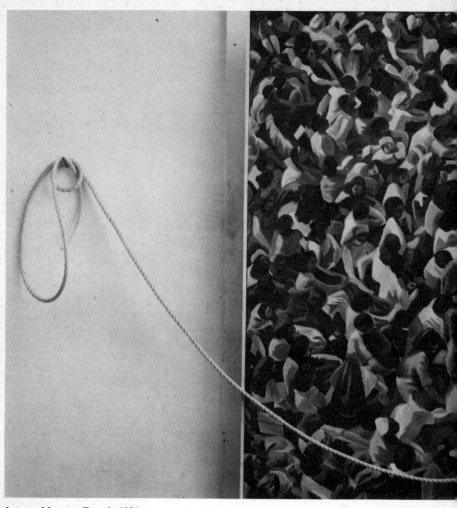

Jacques Monory, French, 1934-
Comme il vous plaira, 1967
Galerie B. Mommaton, Paris

Antonio Berni, Argentinian, 1905-
La grande illusion, 1962

118

and the poster)? I am, moreover, astonished that none of our opponents has ever used this windfall of a quotation: "Literary and art criticism call for two criteria: one political, the other artistic..."

"And what is the relationship between these two criteria? It is no more possible to put an 'equals' sign between politics and art than between a general concept of the world and the methods of artistic creation and criticism. We deny the existence of an abstract, immutable political criterion; every class in every class society has its own criteria, both political and artistic. Nonetheless, every class in every class society puts the political criterion first and the artistic criterion second... As for us, we demand a unity of politics and art, a unity of form and content, a unity of revolutionary political content and as perfect as possible an artistic form. Works without artistic value, however advanced they may be from the political point of view, remain ineffective. That is why we are against works of art that express erroneous political views and also against the tendency to produce works in the 'slogan and poster style' which are correct in their political views but are weak in artistic expression. We must, in literature and art, conduct the struggle on two fronts."

Mao Tse-tung is apparently reacting against the abuses inherent in every revolutionary explosion when communication runs ahead of the medium and the content ahead of the form. The passage constitutes a partial condemnation of Jdanovism and the authoritarian standardization of visual norms (the rejection of the entire western school from Impressionism onwards) although the concept of "power of artistic expression" which he uses is left extremely vague. Who nowadays, apart from a few retarded academicians in Moscow and elsewhere, can approve this dictatorship in literary and artistic creation which the young Yugoslav writer Miroslav Krleza has been denouncing since 1952 for its desire to submit the arts "to the political will pure and simple, in the fanatical, one-sided form of the spirit of the party..." However, let us be quite clear that the conditions for liberty of intention and execution are almost always preserved in revolutionary art, for the reason that this art goes against the stream and is the object of hostility on the part of the existing power structure and scorn on the part of the fashionable headquarters, namely the network of galleries and museums that make and unmake the art market; things move differently in a given society when power changes hands. From being a revolutionary art it runs the risk of becoming a congratulatory art, and the shadow of a new "socialist realism" soon begins to form. If the example of Cuba is entirely positive on this point, it is because the artists enjoy, as we have noted, total freedom of conception, and the identification with the socialist struggle is made in a climate of urgency and enthusiasm. The worst that can happen to a revolutionary painter is not so much his submitting, through laziness or necessity, to the pressures of a dealer in a capitalist society as to become, in a socialist society, a blind thurifer of the regime, a spokesman for integration, a man who has ceased to keep a vigilant eye on the world he is helping to construct, and all this through submission to a discipline and an ideology.

My last point is, does painting as confrontation exist? This question is hardly a paradox, for the limits of confrontation must be continually redefined, and we have seen that its field of action is very extensive. It would be presumptuous for a painter to lay permanent claim to a revolutionary status and to reduce his art to nothing but a tedious machine for negation. Among the artists we exhibited at "The World in Question," some, as far as their art was concerned, had only adopted a political stance two or three times in their lives (Crémonini), others had created a number of works that were eloquent as political statements (Matta), or confined themselves to a slow work of undermining (Berni).

These divergences in the nature of the confrontation, which may occur as a response to the occasional promptings of conscience or to an urge of longer duration, only add to our uncertainties. In any case, no one can arrogate to himself the right to design this or that, to distribute certificates of political involvement, and it is a field in which the attempt at investigation clashes as much with the resistance within ourselves as with the resistance that is offered us by the world we live in.

1. Animation Research Confrontation — Section directed by Pierre Gaudibert.
2. Cf. Opus international, No. 7, p. 78.

Raymonde Moulin

Living without selling

Merchandise will be burned
Censier

Twenty years before the May Revolution, the following statement was written by a liberal economist: "The entire capitalist society functions regularly thanks to some social sectors that are not animated by the spirit of profit and the search for the greatest gain. When the high official, the magistrate, the artist, and the intellectual become dominated by this spirit, society crumbles and the entire economic order is threatened."[1] The existence of the work of art as merchandise, the dominant role assumed by the market in the organization of artistic life, the subjection of artists to restrictions that are inherent in the logic of the economy, all this was inevitably contested in a far more radical way by the revolutionaries of May 1968. Could those who despise capitalist society, the consumer society, forego such an appropiate occasion to emphasize the encroachment of financial monopolies on creative activity and to denounce the hypocrisy of an ideology that sanctifies art, glorifies artists, and portrays the relationship between the art lover and the work of art as a pure, disinterested love, while concealing the fact that works of art are the subject of commercial deals? The dignity that our society recognizes in art constitutes one side of a system, of which the reverse is commercialization in art. This we already knew. Nonetheless, with many, the spirit of resignation outweighed that of revolt, and the pessimists affirmed that there is no instance of an organization that excludes all form of restriction and assures the creative artist liberty and security. The revolutionaries of the École des Beaux-Arts and various art committees systematically made an issue of what was commonly admitted, namely the economic status of the work of art, the market system, and the ambiguous position of the artist as both creator of esthetic objects and producer of goods to be sold. To understand the meaning and import of this issue, it is essential to bear in mind the main aspects of the

121

system that was contested. We shall then examine the ideas that sprang up or sprang up anew amid the delicious fever and lyric effusion that seized artistic circles in May 1968. To what extent was the behavior of the various participants determined by bitterness, resentment, noble enthusiasm, or strategic prudence? To what extent were their proposals and suggestions determined by negative criticism, creative utopianism, or daydreams?

It is perfectly clear that art has always had a price. Works of art, like precious stones and pearls, like rare objects, have served in all mercantile societies as "refuges" for rich men who are anxious to safeguard their fortunes or their speculative investments. Works of art are extraordinary goods whose special nature has been recognized by economists from Ricardo to Karl Marx and John Stuart Mill. Unique, irreplaceable, a thing of virtually indestructible enjoyment (for contemplation of it does not change it), a work of art is defined economically in contrast to durable and non-durable consumer goods, which are essentially destined to destruction. Unless a museum steps in, the unique work of art is normally an article of private acquisition and enjoyment, conferring prestige and constituting an investment. As an easily movable article of furniture, the easel picture lends itself readily to secret financial manipulations. Like gold, it falls into the category of investments without yield; however, unlike gold, it may not be the object of transactions on the stock market, but only financial transactions through private sale or at auction. In the course of these transactions, the work of art is evaluated in terms of price, and these prices can only be established on the market.

Art dealing and speculation have existed in all societies in which there is individual artistic creation and an art clientele of individuals, in which art no longer caters to the needs of the group, as in primitive societies, but has become the property and the means of enjoyment, if not the instrument of power, of a minority. The influence on the artist's condition exercised by the traffic in art varies, however, according to the organization of artistic life, which can be understood only in relation to the social complex that makes it possible. It was in nineteenth-century France that the picture market began to rely on the academic system to ensure the diffusion of art, the recognition of works, and a means of livelihood for the artist. From the moment when the contract for an as yet unexecuted work bound the artist to the dealer like the writer to the publisher, the circulation process was transformed, to use a Marxist term, into a process of production, and from being an "unproductive" worker, the artist is transformed into a "productive worker," for he produces capital. The direct, personal relationship of the artist to the devotee which prevailed in the age of private patronage has been replaced by the direct relationship of the artist to the dealer; imperative command has been replaced by the insidious restrictions known as demand. "The crux of the matter," Van Gogh wrote to his brother Théo, "is that my possibilities of work depend on the sale of my work... Not to sell, when you have no resources, makes it impossible for you to progress, whereas progress would come of itself if these circumstances were changed."[2] From the moment when the dealer became the champion of a work of art and assured its commercial success, when the market became an open structure to the exclusion of the official salon, artists have had the feeling that they have won their independence. But by breaching official absolutism and freeing themselves from the academic system, artists had scarcely gained this independence when they forfeited it in a market system which became more and more efficient but also, in view of the priority given to the economic goal, more oppressive for them.

In the last hundred years the capitalist system has increasingly commandeered the art market. Since the Second World War, monopolistic elements have been predominant. Every artist has the monopoly of his production, and at the outset has the sole right to offer it for sale. He can sell his work to collectors directly or else through an intermediary. In the latter case he can grant or refuse his distributor a monopoly on the sale of his "production"; he can discriminate between dealers by granting one the right of first refusal or else treat them all equally.[3] The least imperfect image of monopolistic mechanisms is given by the most speculative sector of the market, provided it is observed from a static point of view. The temporarily monopolistic dealer is master of the price. He works with a restricted number of collectors who aim to hoard, and their financial potential is considerable. Each restricted commercial circuit that revolves around an artist is not to be thought of as the mob (as is feared by those who are aware of the hypothetical nature of esthetic value), but at the very least as a supreme form of monopoly typified by, in the economic sense of the term, a coalition. A dynamic worldwide analysis of the contemporary art market reveals, however, how the monopolistic set-up has been subverted and competitive practices have been introduced.

Competition exists at the level of the "product"; the market is full of tensions, for great artistic controversies and economic rivalries assert themselves one against the other. Each of the chief contestants—painter, dealer, critic and collector—fights for recognition of the art he has produced or has chosen to champion.

In certain essential sectors of modern life, the scientific organization of labor, the controlled distribution of investment, and social planning tend to reduce the effects of merciless competition; but the art world is going through a stage of individualistic creation in which the artist is deified, and is hence a Darwinian jungle in which each artist offers, or believes he offers, a universe that is incompatible with those of his fellows. There is also price competition because of the "parallel market," that is to say that sector of the market that eludes the monopolistic dealers and is controlled by middlemen, brokers, and collector-dealers. Enthusiasts who are quick to spot talent and acquire pictures at very low prices, as well as brokers who sell at special rates in galleries, can reintroduce works of art into the commercial circuit at very competitive prices. The price dictated by the dealer who keeps the supply in check and thus stimulates demand can't help seeming arbitrary when compared with the "parallel market" and public auctions. His price is determined by supply and demand, both of which are rigged; the former is engineered by the supplier in terms of tactical requirements (it is clear that the interests of the distributor don't necessarily coincide with those of the artist); the latter is subjected to various psychological pressures, among which must be counted the subtlest forms of publicity.

The structure and workings of the art market reflect the tangle of cultural values and economic interests in our social system. In the last analysis, the condition of the artist depends on this market. Let us compare the different forms of society in which he is placed: in the U.S.S.R., painting is subject to ideology and the artist's career is institutionalized; pupils at the State Schools are selected at the age of twelve to receive, together with a general education, specialized art instruction which prepares them for the entrance examination to the School of Fine Arts at the age of eighteen. On leaving the School they become teachers or are admitted to the artists' union and devote themselves entirely to painting; higher and higher distinctions are open to them, culminating in membership in the Academy of Fine Arts. In the United States there is neither a National School of Fine Arts nor an Academy. Artists are trained in privately run schools and their works are exhibited in private galleries or in museums that generally are endowed institutions. The development of their careers depends on their success with their clientele. To put matters simply, on one side we have a career of submission to an ideology and judicious assessment of official requirements and on the other a free, commercial career.

In France, freedom of artistic creation is assured. But when we look behind this principle, we find that the two kinds of career coexist: the official career that leads to the Academy of Fine Arts and the free career that is ultimately sanctioned by economic selection on the part of the market. The difference between these two types of career is today one of principle rather than fact. The organization of the academic system ensures a closed circle—the co-opting of academicians, the quasi-monopoly of teaching and awards, particularly the *Prix de Rome*, and the selection of academicians from among the winners of the great competitions. It was in opposition to this closed structure that the system of dealers came about at the end of the nineteenth century. In the course of the last twenty years, however, the prizes awarded by international juries, as at the great biennales, have come to mark the normal stages in a painter's career. Non-academic art has its medalists; and new mandarins (the product of an alternative official channel) have superseded the outcasts. On the other hand, it would doubtless be misleading to contrast the great international juries with juries of professors unfamiliar with commerce and prisoner of their esthetic traditions. Academic art has not escaped being the servant of commerce, and persons of influence in this market have multiplied the awarding of prizes by juries that are recruited in a diversity of ways. This is to say that the present situation lacks neither complexity nor ambiguity, and the two types of career influence each other reciprocally: the academic career opens into the commercial career, and the free career, which is predominantly commercial, tends to become institutionalized. The route leading to honors is foreseeable in both cases, and the tests to be passed are clearly charted. In both types of career, honors affect prices, nor does one always know whether economic pressure groups did not originate the distinction: "*Pretium* means on the one hand *pretium justum*, the medieval equivalent of the modern concept of market value, and on the other hand it also means praise and honor."[4] Recognition by the restricted group, national or international, of those who establish the hierarchical classification of painters and the ability to command high prices are the artist's two criteria of success, constantly interacting, each attesting the other.

If the artist is to ensure his existence, he can't ignore the dealer, the critic, demand, publicity, or the hazards of the economy. Even if artists object to the appreciation they receive from the market, it is no less true that the relation of the artist to his work is affected by his relation to the external world. The relation of the creator to his creation cannot be independent of the idea that others form of his work, and the price paid for it.

If the hold of trade on the diffusion of art is such that esthetic judgment is devalued in proportion as commercial manipulation occurs, all esteem becomes equivocal, and the satisfaction of being a high-priced artist does not exclude resentment over the means of success, or uneasiness over its significance. The fact that the recognition of an artist arrives via the market is the clearest evidence of his alienation in western societies; creators flounder between two types of limitation according to the nature of the work accomplished and their own capacity for integration within a competitive system. The brutal restrictions caused by difficulty in selling impede the very realization of the creative project. The insidious coercion of commercial success may incite the artist to steer his project in the direction of demand. Two phases are discernible in the post-war period: until 1962 the euphoria of the market was such that the coercions associated with success were particularly apparent; the sickness that followed gave rise to compulsions that arose from insecurity. And since alienation through poverty is unquestionably more unbearable than alienation through wealth, artists modified their way of life.

In the fifties, the art trade saw exceptional prosperity, and the support given to the avant-garde by part of the buying public led to the belief that a new golden age was opening for artists. I do not intend to dwell at length on the circumstances that worked in favor of high prices. The general economic situation (growth accompanied by inflation), speculation encouraged by the absence of a capital gains tax, and the special prestige conferred on bourgeois art collectors, who sought to acquire an aristocratic image by the possession of works of art, all acted in the market's favor. The spread of the monopoly contract has exercised an influence in the same direction; what dealer would have taken the risk of a large financial outlay to ensure the rapid rise of an artist to a position of commercial success if he had not first obtained exclusive rights to that artist's production? The speculative fever of the fifties, plus financial and publicity techniques, assured the promotion of the most recent art styles and led people to believe that a work of art could be treated as an ordinary piece of merchandise. The most representative dealers at this privileged moment in the history of the market exploited their opportunities to the hilt. By bulling the market, they awakened a keen interest in contemporary art, assured their impatient artists (who were often their accomplices) of a quick commercial success, and brought considerable profit to those collectors who thought of pictures as stocks and shares. During these same years the prosperity of the market gave artists a relative security, while some made sizable fortunes. Van Gogh could sell only one picture in his life. Artists born around 1900 achieved commercial success at the age of fifty. Artists born around 1920 could more easily reach the same point in thirty or forty years. Many of them managed to adapt (without any apparent psychological trauma) to a system that puts economics first and gives a competitive character to the relationship between individuals and groups of interests. The euphoria of the market coincided with the "end of the revolt" on the part of the artists. It was possible to believe, without going against the facts, that the reconciliation of liberty and security was possible.

Since 1962, the climate of euphoria has been succeeded by one of prudence, even defiance. In the markets where psychological factors are dominant, speculative fever and a boom summon, as their inevitable counterpart, panic and a slump. There was a touch of imprudence in allowing the prices of contemporary works to rise too high, so that the threat of overproduction (unknown in the market for old masters) hovers over the market for works by living artists. Speculation on a rise in prices could only lead to the collapse of the market. On the other hand, the sickness that hit the Bourse after 1963 profoundly changed the speculative sector of the art market which deals in recent works; as for other works of dependable value as investments, they continued to rise. When the Bourse drops, the dynamic army of speculative collectors adopts a position of retreat. Finally, the Americans who used to be the great buyers on the French art market not only have begun to buy American works but even to impose the New York School on Europeans. It is in this context of economic stagnation that the great query implied by the market system has reappeared: if the prosperity of the market is in doubt, what becomes of the artist's security, and if he has no security can he still count on his liberty?

At the moment of the explosion of May 1968, the situation in the French art market was disturbing, and this seems to have been a by no means negligible contributing factor. Since the 1870s; which saw the creation of the market system as a system for organizing the world of art, the anxiety of the artist has disappeared or been only latent in phases of prosperity, but it has appeared in times of crisis (e.g. the financial disasters of 1884 and the recession of the thirties). It is at such moments that the system is called into question and radical solutions are the order of the day. It is the same in the sixties. We must not forget the objective difficulties created by the general situation, but apart from that the cooperative formula that had fed the dreams of Van Gogh found its adherents. The easel picture, an ideal object of private acquisition, was challenged, as in the thirties, by the champions of a monumental art that could serve as a framework for the life of the community. Finally, the invention of multiples seemed bound to lead to a radical transformation of the social and

127

economic status of the work of art. Once we admit that the concept of the multiple implies the utilization of industrial techniques as a means of creation and not of reproduction, the elimination of the original, and the manufacture in series of indentical, interchangeable objects, abundance replaces rarity and works of art thus lose both their exceptional dignity and their quality as extraordinary economic goods. Behind various artistic experiments can be found a desire on the part of the artist to work not for the culturally and financially privileged, but for the whole of society, whether by participating in large architectural schemes or putting works of art (now categorized as reproductive goods) within the financial reach of the majority. The various proposals as to what to do about art are apt to call the reigning ideology into question, and they do not allow us to dodge the problem of economic fluctuations. Monumental art is not outside the capitalist economy, and those artists who have been induced to join architects in developing such works remain subject to the cultural, social, financial, and administrative demands that in our society are inherent in any commission. The multiple must either be marketed in art galleries of the traditional type or else be condemned to the economic outlets of widely diffused cultural goods (such as records and books) or gadgets.

None of the recent concrete efforts to extricate artistic production from the closed circle of the galleries has succeeded in freeing it from its integral place within the economy. All that has changed is the mode of economization, and this is due to the very nature of recent esthetic research. The May revolutionaries directed their attack against the whole society, arguing on an abstract plane and making (at least partially) an abstraction of their respective esthetic choices, so they could go much further in their confrontation of the existing institutions and of the prevailing ideology, and such was the impetus of their creative aspiration that they sought to elaborate an alternative ideology and propose alternative institutions.

The confrontation of the art market implies, in the first instance, the confrontation of the economic status of the work of art. Its degradation into an article of merchandise, the subjection of the creator to the logic of the economy, and the degeneration of the art lover into a speculator have made it ethically displeasing. On the one hand, the moral condemnation of the power of money is not of recent origin, and in some excellent pages of the *Manuscripts of 1844*,[5] Marx does not hesitate to quote Goethe and Shakespeare; on the other hand, revolution is hopeless unless accompanied by a fervent, rigorous aspiration towards purity. The anxiety to avoid the contamination of money was evident in the indignant refusal of the May revolutionaries to market the posters issued by the popular studio at the École des Beaux-Arts. They didn't, however, confine themselves to a rediscovery of Marx's ethical preoccupations; their outlook was influenced by the theory in *Das Kapital* that the problem is one of merchandise fetishism and the servitude of the "salaried" artist, whose production is subordinated from the outset to capital and exists only for its profit. And it is doubtless because the May revolutionaries placed themselves more or less consciously in a Marxist perspective that they attacked the system rather than individuals—denunciations of the personal practices of this or that dealer were not frequent, and there were no broken windows.

The attack was directed no less against the social status of the work of art than against its economic status, each being seen as a reinforcement of the other. A doubly elitist concept of esthetic consumption as the privilege of the inheritors of culture, money, or both was contrasted with a democratic concept, implying equality in the right to have art. The exercise of this right necessitates that art education[6] should not be left to the family circle and that if the diffusion of art is not confined to a happy few, every social stratum can be reached by it.[7]

The double rejection we have just been considering implied a third: the rejection of the condition imposed on the artist by industrial capitalist society. The objections were not confined to the influence that honors and prices have on each other, that is to say the confusion between esthetic and financial value. Both honors and prices were condemned as such; the "mandarin" had to be annihilated, whether as the superstar of the international market or the pontiff of the École des Beaux-Arts in Paris. The elimination of all hierarchies went hand in hand with the rejection of competitive selection, whether by the expedient of examinations or of competition.

The attack on institutions was motivated in part by the impetuous fervor for demystification. A society dominated by the profit motive and yet anxious to safeguard the purity of its cultural values justifies itself by ideologies that inevitably call for inspection. The ideology of creative liberty, which has been cultivated as much by the system's outcasts as by its elect, was denounced in Marxist terms, i.e. it could only be an illusion in a society in which art is the monopoly of the ruling classes. "Secondly, my dear bourgeois individualists, we must inform you that your talk of absolute liberty is nothing but sheer hypocrisy. In a society founded on the power of money, in a society whose laboring masses exist in misery while the wealthy few live as parasites, there can be no real 'liberty'... And it's up to us socialists to unmask this hypocrisy, let us tear down

129

these false banners, not to bring about a literature and art that are outside class (that will only be possible in a classless socialist society), but to replace a literature that hypocritically claims to be free and is in fact bound to the bourgeoisie, by a literature that claims to be free and is overtly bound to the proletariat."[8]

The ideology of art for art's sake was attacked in terms that were reminiscent of Proudhon and Plekhanov:

> "We are against the ruling force of our day. What is the ruling force of our day? Bourgeois art and bourgeois culture.
>
> What is bourgeois culture? It is the instrument whereby the ruling class's power of oppression accords artists a privileged status so as to separate and isolate them from all other workers. This privilege locks the artist in an invisible prison. The fundamental concepts underlying this isolating action that the culture exerts are:
>
> — The idea that art has achieved autonomy (Malraux: see his lecture on the occasion of the Olympic Games in Grenoble).
> — The defense of 'freedom of creation.' Culture gives the artist an illusion of liberty:
>
> 1. He makes what he pleases, he believes everything is possible, he is accountable only to himself and to Art.
>
> 2. He is a 'creator,' that is to say he invents totally something unique whose value is permanent and above historical reality. He is not a worker at grips with historical reality. The idea of creation makes his work an unreality.
>
> By allotting the artist a privileged status, culture renders him harmless and functions as a safety-valve in the mechanism of bourgeois society.
>
> This is the situation in which we all find ourselves. We are all bourgeois artists. How could it be otherwise? That is why we use the term 'popular studio,' for there is no question of reform but of a *radical change in orientation.*
>
> I.e., we have decided to transform what we are in society."[9]

Thus the charismatic ideology of the artist, which came into being with Renaissance humanism, to be confirmed and sublimated by romanticism and carried to its logical extreme by the theoreticians of art for art's sake, has at last been repudiated. Artists are no longer quasi-gods who exist outside the norms of the community. They have been seized by an almost mystical fever of renunciation: "I renounce my status as an artist"; "the artist must melt into anonymity." Painters, from the most illustrious to the most obscure, would no doubt have been capable of indulging in that ultimate self-effacement that was given theatrical formulation by Jean-Louis Barrault: "Jean-Louis Barrault is dead." But like the Trappist who forgets himself to become engulfed in God, the artist denied himself so as to melt into collectivity, to become one with the people by working for society as a whole:

> "Let us escape from the condition of the isolated Artist, who remains on the periphery of the realities of the street, the city, and everyday surroundings, creating images that are never integrated because they are destined for museums and the apartments of the rich, because they are articles of mercantile value or items for archives, cultural certificates, because their authority is probably conditioned by the cult of personality and signature, a trap laid by confidence tricksters.
>
> Let us put an end to this age-old definition of the artist that is handed down by dealers, schools, and institutes... Let us infiltrate the community with the plastic means at our disposal and create activities on a human scale."[10]

The temptation of self-criticism spared neither all the dealers nor all the art critics. There can be no doubt that some of them thereby found a means of expressing their bad consciences; it is not always without a certain pang that dealers reconcile, in their daily experience, the love of art and the pursuit of money, or that critics transform themselves into impresarios. Those who were most aware of the vices within the system and most irrational in their sympathy with the artists' revolt were ready to dig their own graves. Twenty-four dealers (some out of conviction, others out of opportunism) signed a carefully weighed declaration that recognized art's power of confrontation without confronting the existing means of its diffusion:

> "The undersigned directors of galleries of contemporary art reaffirm their full and complete solidarity with those artists whose purpose has always been confrontation by means of their creative activity and hereby affirm their solidarity with the struggle of the students and workers.
>
> They are determined to continue their activity and to intensify their dialogue with artists and students of different creative and educational disciplines and generally with all who are concerned with art.

131

They undertake:

1. To help all the artists with whom they are in contact in their task of making posters on behalf of the movement.
2. To distribute and sell these posters exclusively for the profit of this struggle.

Ariel – Henri Benezit – Breteau – Cimaise Bonaparte – Cl. Bernard – La Demeure – Le Dragon – Lucien Durand – Paul Fachetti – Mathias Fels – Jean Fournier – Galerie de France – Daniel Gervis – La Hune – Beno d'Incelli – Jeanne Bucher – Maeght – Jacques-Henry Perrin – Camille Renault – Schoeller – 3 + 2 – Vercamer – Villand Galanis – Lara Vinci."

If the criticism of the market and the reigning ideology was nourished on references, implicit or explicit, to Marxism, the revolutionaries of May 1968 did not ignore the avatars of Soviet socialist realism or the doctrinaire demands of Jdanovism. This is doubtless the reason why they reached an ideological syncretism in which the surrealist ingredient was no less important than the Marxist. The bitter skepticism of Dada, which led to an art movement and finally an attempt at total negation, inspired the vengeful project smelling of nihilism that was directed against culture, against the instrument of its trans-mission—the university—and against its conservatories—the museums. The defense of chance and the pure flow of spontaneity, the exaltation of blinding love, and the desire to re-establish man's primordial relationship with the universe and achieve a psychological revolution by utilizing that particular form of action known as artistic creation, have abundantly demonstrated that the thought of André Breton has permeated the age. The May revolutionaries tried, without succumbing other than symbolically to the temptation, to revive on their own account the anarchist nostalgia of the surrealist movement."

The "hordes of words"[12] that were let loose in May 1968 dealt with both Marxist and surrealist themes, though this statement is a deceptive simplification. The originality of the May revolutionaries lay in the fact that they were "definitive dreamers"[13] or genuine prophets: they conceived the possibility of reconciling practical revolutionary politics and creative liberty—a reconciliation that André Breton had considered impossible.

If we turn from the manifestos of the May revolutionaries to their behavior, we find that the contradictions remain. The surrealist attitude simply prevailed over the Marxist attitude. For a good number of revolutionary artists as well as for a good number of students, the confrontation was a poetic experience:

"Under the paving-stones, the beach." Revolution, like life, is an art, and it is up to each of us to live it like an artist. To elevate the paving-stone into a work of art, as some actually did, is to place oneself in the tradition of Marcel Duchamp rather than that of Lenin. To conceive revolution as a liberating festivity, as a sort of gigantic happening, demanding the participation of everyone and snatching the actors from the passivity and glumness of the commonplace, is to be an artist practicing the art of changing the world by changing life, and this is fairly far removed from the classic Marxist model. If we re-read Marx's antithetical descriptions of bourgeois revolutions and proletarian revolutions, we find that the May revolution fits more readily into the former category: "Bourgeois revolutions, like those of the eighteenth century, sweep headlong from success to success, their dramatic effects are ever greater, men and things seem to be caught in a fire of diamonds, ecstatic enthusiasm is the permanent state of society, but they are of short duration. They quickly reach their culminating point, and a lengthy sickness seizes society before it learns to adapt itself calmly and soberly to the results of its stormy period."[14]

The ideological program that artistic circles worked out in May 1968 attempted to combine (not without a certain glorious confusion) the Marxist critique of capitalist society, the Dadaist rejection of the legitimacy of culture and the legitimacy of boredom, and the surrealist aspiration to all forms of liberation. The revolutionary artists opposed the restrictions exercised by the market, but they were no less hostile to the ideological slavery that threatens creativity in socialist societies. They claim security all the more insistently for having sensed their vulnerability, the sale of pictures being at the mercy of agents, economic crises, and the incomprehension of the consumers. But they would not be prepared to pay for security at the expense of freedom, in the western sense of the word, even though the latter may have struck them as singularly precarious in the course of the heated debates of May 1968. The artists knew what they no longer wanted, and what they didn't want. The transition from this ethic (or esthetic) of rejection to the establishment of alternative institutions evidently had its difficulties.

The magnitude of the contradictions to be surmounted appeared (and this is only one example) in connection with the democratization of art education. Do we want everyone to have access to culture or must culture be destroyed? "To reproach the houses of culture with not having reached the non-public is to admit the importance of those values that should be communicated to all. To consider these values bourgeois and to suppose that they will cease to be bourgeois when universality of access comes to coincide with universality of rights is contradictory."[15]   To resolve the problem by proposing an education that "develops creativity" is to "Montessorize" art education (which is not without its pedagogic interest), it is to advance the comforting hypothesis that a creator lies dormant in every individual, it is to assimilate art for all into art *by* all.

The commission that was charged with investigating the status of the professional creator proscribed the term artist and suggested the assimilation of the ex-artist's situation into that of the research worker.   State grants would give creators in the visual arts the same support as is received by scientific research workers.   Although the identification of the artist with the research worker strikes us as bearing the mark of a rationalized, scientific, technological society, it does have its advantages—the artist, like the scientist, would escape at least partially from the market.[16]   The month of May 1968 was long enough for the promoters of the revolution in the artist's status to grasp the difficulties.   Will everyone who feels he has an artistic vocation be taken in charge by the State?   Clearly not.   At the moment, no society has reached a level of affluence that would allow it to guarantee the livelihood of all those who, if only to relieve their neuroses, feel the desire to paint or sculpture.   The status of research worker does not get us out of the trap of selection.   Who will be the judges that are considered competent to choose the artists due for a state salary, and what are the criteria by which they will judge?   The month of May 1968 was not long enough for the answers to this set of queries to be properly formulated.   There is a chance, however, that constructive thought in this field will survive the revolutionary Spring.

All the themes that were debated in revolutionary art circles, and there were many of them, as well as the solutions that were envisaged, could not leave two historical facts out of account.   Except for the short-lived *Proletkult*, there is no example to show that revolutionary art was that of revolutionaries. This was so true in May 1968 that, in the meetings and committees where academic artists, surrealists, and the exponents of kinetic art, Pop Art, or politically committed realism came together in one great revolutionary brotherhood, esthetics took a back seat.   Politics, economics, and sociology were discussed, but from the outset there was a moratorium on esthetic controversy.   It was a sacred truce, yet unquestionably a provisional one.   Nor does history offer any example of a society that has lastingly resolved the following contradiction: what the artist gains in security he loses in liberty.   The revolutionaries didn't dream of denying this; there was no model on which they could fasten, for they rejected simultaneously the American artist's condition and that of the Soviet artist and the French artist, for the last of whom they saw rather the combination of drawbacks than the accumulation of advantages. Some evoked the Cuban celebrations or the exploits of the Chinese Cultural Revolution, but in their view the artist's paradise existed nowhere. Paradise is to come, in a future society that will have changed the world as Marx wanted, and changed life as Rimbaud and Breton hoped, in a society that will have reconciled its aspirations. The rational observer will maintain that to take the best from each system while omitting the social context that has made it possible, to hanker nostalgically after the kind of patronage exercised by American foundations and at the same time to strive for socialist egalitarianism, and to take "the right side of the material" of each type of society while rejecting the "wrong" side, is to fall victim to utopianism. He will observe that as far as France and the present moment are concerned, the explosion of May 1968 aggravated the economic difficulties, while the artist, who today as yesterday is condemned to sell in order to live, finds himself in a situation that has been in no way simplified. The revolutionaries, whose passion has assuredly prevailed over their reason—but after all, no great achievement has ever been realized without passion—continue to nourish exultant hopes for a society that will allow them to dissociate art from economics and from bourgeois culture and associate it with the life of a society that will authorize them to burn art insofar as it is merchandise and the object of veneration, a society that will offer the artist an opportunity to be free, to live without selling.

1. François PERROUX, *Le Capitalisme*, Paris, Presses Universitaires de France, 1948, p. 103.

2. Vincent VAN GOGH, *Lettres à son frère Théo*, Paris, Gallimard, 1956, p. 271.

3. Cf. Raymonde MOULIN, *Le marché de la peinture en France*, Paris, Les Éditions de Minuit, 1967, Ch. 7.

4. J. HUIZINGA, *Homo ludens*, an essay on the social function of games, Paris, Gallimard, 1951, p. 92.

5. Karl MARX, *Manuscrits de 1844*, Les Éditions Sociales, pp. 119-123.

6. For a criticism of the ideology that "entirely abandons every hope of cultural health to the inscrutable workings of grace, or rather, talent," the reader is invited to refer to *L'Amour de l'Art*, by Pierre BOURDIEU, Alain DARBE, and Dominique SCHNAPPER, Paris, Les Éditions de Minuit, 1966.

7. "We must replace the culture that is only realizable by those who have been formed to it from a very early age... We shall have to destroy the commercial network for the distribution of works of art that exists solely for speculation and for an elite." (École des Beaux-Arts, Commission on: Reform of instruction in the plastic arts.)

8. LENIN, "The organization of the Party and the literature of the Party." *Novaia Jizn* (New life), November 13 (26), 1905.

9. Manifesto issued by the popular studio of the École des Beaux-Arts: *Atelier populaire "oui," atelier bourgeois "non."*

10. This text was posted on the Maison des Beaux-Arts, 11 rue des Beaux-Arts, Paris V[e].

11. "The simplest surrealist act consists in going down into the street with revolvers in hand and firing at random into the crowd. Any person who hasn't at least once wanted in this way to put an end to the present petty system of degradation and cretinization has his appointed place in that crowd with a cannon aimed at his stomach." André BRETON, *Second manifeste du surréalisme*, Paris, Collection Idées. 1965, p. 78.

12. The expression is borrowed from André Breton.

13. Op. cit.

14. Karl MARX, *Les luttes de classe en France 1848-50*, Paris, Pauvert, 1965, p. 224.

15. Gaétan PICON, "Confrontation and culture," *Le Monde*, August 6, 1968.

16. Although there exists a market for scientific research.

Pierre Gaudibert

The cultural world and art education

In May and June 1968, there arose a sudden vast questioning of the "entire structure of artistic life in France." In the wake of the student confrontation, the movement spread both spontaneously and in response to the student union that demanded the extension of the struggle to the cultural area. This is to say that the artists who participated in large numbers and in very different ways in this moral and political insurrection went beyond such merely corporate demands as aimed at improving the existing system by better working conditions and greater professional security (old age benefits, social security, studios, etc...)

An essential dimension of artistic life was revealed from the outset with stunning clarity, namely that of the *existing system*, which was no longer accepted as part of the natural order of things, compelling everyone to shift for himself if he was to continue to produce, but as a social complex that could be collectively confronted. If architects, for example, had already experienced their "architectural act" as a political act because it was hemmed in on all sides by social pressures and restrictions, the conscience of the painter and the sculptor was in a more uneven and hazy state. It was at first through this discovery that part of the artistic community became a radical political force; everyone could join others, in spite of all the difficulties, in trying to make inroads on the existing structures, whether they were those of his own socio-professional field or those of society as a whole.

An awareness of the objective existence of a *cultural field*, which is always present in the relationship between an artistic producer and his work (while his subjectivity gives him the illusion of an immediate relationship) became an irreversible experience that could not be obliterated by a return to "order." The artists' "invisible cage" that Che Guevara spoke of in *Socialism and Man in*

137

Cuba became apparent to them at the very moment when they could, it seemed, have a hold over it. Thus a pre-revolutionary situation and a new collective experience joined with concepts that had been elaborated by a critical cultural sociology and a problematical Marxist[1].

If we tried to sum up in as simple a way as possible the concept of the cultural domain insofar as it involves the visual arts, we would have to say that we are concerned with a system of social relations in which each agent or group of agents is defined by its position in relation to the whole—a whole that is never the simple addition of the juxtaposed parts. Instead of setting up works of art as esthetic objects to be studied in terms of their structure and significance (the history of art or the sociology of art), we take them for "products," "goods," "merchandise" that circulate on the market. Their role is that of turntables around which gravitate the producers, or "artists," at one extreme, while at the other are the consumers or receivers, the clientele and the public.

The two poles of this complex network are related to one another by means of a host of intermediaries who ensure both the economic and the cultural promotion of works of art (the circuit of dealers and speculators, academies, museums, houses of culture, administrative bodies for the fine arts, art critics, etc...). Seen in its entirety, this constitutes, with its own peculiar logic, an instance of selection, distribution, reception, and legitimation. It creates value in two senses of the term: it determines the hierarchy of esthetic values in contemporary art and ensures its degree of economic success by variations of price on the art market.

The ties that relate the positions of the different protagonists in this field lend it a certain coherence, which in turn creates a relative autonomy in relation to society as a whole and determines its own mode of evolution—that which permits us to speak of *structure* and *system* without falling into pure intellectual snobbery. All the participants in this field (though opposed to each other by virtue of individual rivalry) and all the socio-professional categories and subcategories it comprises are concerned with its existence and proper functioning; attitudes of rejection, revolt, and peripheral withdrawal are only defined in implicit or explicit relationship to this social reality.

Historically speaking, several socio-cultural systems that concern the visual arts have succeeded one another or overlapped within the same historically determined social structure, with varying degrees of relative autonomy. The prevailing system of our own day came into being around the 1880s under the impact of decisive changes in the way the dealers' network functioned, and since then it has continually developed, with the increasing roles of, among others, publicity and speculation. This is the dominant system as against the academic system and what could be called "small-scale production" in which the art producer is an independent artisan who himself takes care of the commercialization of his products.

The logic of the system that at present prevails induces the art producer to turn his back on this objective field so that he may think of himself as a "creator," having at his disposal a limitless power in actions that are sovereignly free and demiurgic. The artist's natural tendency is therefore to preserve an implicit awareness of this field and to refuse to examine it in such an objective way as would enable him to take up a position within it. May and June 1968 saw the dissipation of this illusion and a clarification of the conditions under which "creative liberty" can be exercised.

Moreover, as a cultural field is only relatively autonomous, the recent crisis revealed strategic nodal points at which this field remained in a state of dependence on larger structures, on the whole complex of societal relationships; in the particular case of the visual arts, as in the general case of all the artistic disciplines, these two points were the *market* and the *power structure*. The art market regulates the distribution of works of art as well as their standing, which ensures their promotion; the power structure holds the greater part of the tools that are necessary for an artistic career and imposes its system of cultural reference; these are the two major barriers artists' efforts always come up against. In both these areas the cultivated minority of the bourgeoisie—the class that is economically, politically, and ideologically dominant—controls the fundamental structures of the present system. This is to say that here every reformist measure is quickly stopped short, since any genuine structural reform sets in motion the bourgeoisie's economic and political power. To invent new structures implies a decisive change in societal relationships.

But it so happens that the system which regulates artistic life interacts with another relatively autonomous system that was at the center of the confrontation, the system that regulates the formation of individuals and the transmission of knowledge, namely education. And the system of education has a double impact —in the way it trains the public and in the way it trains the professionals, the future producers of art. In these areas it would seem that there is a greater possibility of radical modifications, in spite of the increasing demands of the profit economy. For some time there has been an ever louder outcry against the inadequacy of art education: insofar there is any, it is sclerotic and archaic.

Several protesting bodies joined forces, thanks to contacts that arose in May and June 1968: artists, students of art history, and former "drawing-masters." There is a flagrant contradiction between a society that implements a policy of cultural action largely concerned with the diffusion of art, that tends therefore to think of art as a social need, and an educational system that assigns it a ridiculously small role as a kind of trivial entertainment. The community as a whole is encouraged to help in the formation and satisfaction of this cultural need, with the support of the State.

Artists have broken with the romantic tradition of the genius who is sublimely indifferent to the reception of his work and convinced of the public's benighted incomprehension; instead they have begun to take an interest in training people's sensibility; beyond the mere presence of works of quality, they are looking toward a pedagogical role which, whether within the framework of the school system or as an outside cultural activity, does not necessarily seem to conflict with their work as artists. Students of art history came to realize not only that there was a shortage of jobs, but also that the university's action in legitimating culture was marred by its reactionary approach—an unconcern with art as it was being made and a continued reference to the values of humanism and the Renaissance. Teachers and students at art schools have become increasingly aware of the scandalous inappropriateness of their instruction and teaching to social requirements and the exigencies of artistic progress in the twentieth century. This convergence of opinion in a field where the possibility of transforming the situation is relatively great has resulted in a large number of proposals and proceedings that the May revolution only increased and radicalized.

Art education

After 1962, the degrading circumstances of art teachers changed for the worse: their pay was low in the extreme, their schedules were reduced, certain posts were discontinued, particularly in Paris, and there was a growing shortage of personnel and equipment. The teaching of drawing, like that of music and manual skills, is accorded neither importance nor dignity in the hierarchy of subjects, and this lack of esteem affects the teachers, who suffer acutely from inequalities in rank and prestige by comparison with other teachers coming out of the university; the optional drawing classes are often scenes of rowdyism; the teacher's views carry little weight in the eyes of the administration unless the teachers in question happen to be well-known artists.

Apart from all these legitimate claims that arose from a deplorable state of affairs, art teachers quickly became aware of the inconsistencies in a fragmented system that developed empirically in the various stages of education. A coherent, unified policy was essential. But only a minority of teachers came to realize that they had received an outmoded training and that it and their teaching methods were equally outmoded by comparison with the upheaval in art since the beginning of the twentieth century, since the majority think, judge, and paint in accordance with the values of traditional painting.

The year 1966 saw the creation of a National Committee for Art Education (CNEA), which regularly published a bulletin and organized displays designed to arouse teachers and public opinion. In 1967 the Ministry decided to create an Arts option for the school-leaving cerificate; unfortunately, however, the decision was not followed up by the necessary steps in high schools. During the preparation of a national colloquium which was to be held at Amiens at the beginning of 1968 on the theme "The training of teachers and educational research," a committee "B" was added to consider "Cultural and art education in the training of the individual." Numerous reports were made at that time and in May and June they were discussed and criticized, particularly those by Charnay, Flocon, Lautrec, and Vigée-Langevin. If we add some new departures in art instruction that remained isolated without being compared with one another and without having any effect on the centers of decision, we can readily understand that many minds were at work in this field when the student confrontation exploded upon France. Those discussions, challenges, and labors expanded into new structures that arose at that time and remained to face the temptation of reformism and its violent rejection by the most radical students, namely the Preparatory Committee for a Remodeling of Art Education (CPREA) and the National Committee of Art Schools. But today everything still remains to be done for this promotion of the arts through education, and it will remain a pious hope if no action is taken.

The traditional school system is entirely based on the unique prestige of the Word, whether spoken or written; from the earliest age the alphabet is taught as a means to both reading and writing, and yet there is no training in the constituent elements of a specific "language" of plastic signs, nothing is done for the "reading" of significant forms, for sensitization to architecture—nothing, that is, for the education of the eye.² Under cover of theories about inborn gifts, which are invoked as justification for the aristocratic establishment, the esthetic sensibility is abandoned to the vagaries of individual chance. This "chance," as Pierre Bourdieu's works have emphasized, in fact consists mainly in the privileges of the social environment into which one is born: those whose childhood is spent in an artistically cultivated environment have benefited by an artistic sensitization by *osmosis*, by a continuous, imperceptible training that can subsequently give the illusion of a gift. The school could be the decisive means of reducing initial inequalities by systematic training. But—and here the fundamental snag lies— it has proved incapable of establishing a basic *alphabetization of forms*.

The essential preliminary for a genuine artistic education (in which the old drawing-master is superseded by the instructor in art education) is a belief in the possible democratization of sensibility and culture by pedagogic means. This further implies a conviction that one of the ends of education is the development of a rich and full personality which is adapted to a world on the move and at the same time is capable of taking the initiative to hasten its transformation; thus the molding of the sensibility becomes a condition of prime importance for this development. That is why, particularly in this field, the noble and humanistic aims that actuate the majority of teachers come up against the exigencies of a profit economy, which wants to make education pay, using it as a factory to turn out the personnel it needs. This is the chief stake in the struggle for education in art, which should be regarded not only as a separate discipline among others, but also as a constant concern, permeating all educational institutions, from kindergarten to university.

Another objective that follows from the preceding is to make the school into the special place for training tomorrow's public, so that that public can actively participate in art while it is being produced. Now this brings us to the second scandal, less unanimously denounced: the elements that are taught within the framework of traditional drawing instruction (thus in the training of future art specialists, producers, teachers, and researchers) are almost completely cut off from the profound change in the entire system of the language of forms which began with the turn of the century and which has proved equal to that of the Renaissance. Drawing instructors, who are themselves the victims of entrance examinations and programs and of their entire outmoded training, are for the most part indifferent or hostile to modern art and give evidence of a conservative attitude. Studios and drawing classes continue to be dependent upon an utterly

142

sclerosed academic training, which in the seventeenth and eighteenth centuries was already a hardened systematization of the artistic conquests of the Renaissance. We all know the importance attached to casts, the antique, copying, perspective, and compositions based on still lifes; these have haunted the scholarly memories of several generations. The result is a huge time-lag between contemporary art and the school system, which does not contribute to the development either of those who are engaged in modern art or of its public; it is at present responsible for the well-known gulf between art and the public that can be said to have yawned since the end of the nineteenth century. Thus the entire system we have been speaking about, which assures the promotion and diffusion of contemporary art, is outside and in opposition to school models, practices, and methods.

Moreover, this species of drawing instruction denies the individual's need for expression, what has been called his "creativity." The sole exception, nowadays universally commended, is the nursery school, which receives children from two to six years of age; under the influence of action methods, Freinet techniques, etc., "free design" has gained ground since the end of World War II. This form of play-activity with brush and paint, which gives free rein to the child's fancy and sensibility, is unfortunately almost never coupled with any training in the artistic vocabulary of our time; hence the child's art disappears without leaving a trace, after having been a collective miracle. By contrast, stultifying restrictions follow, with drawing lessons at the elementary school under well-intentioned but unqualified teachers, creating "a traumatic break" in the development of the child's personality.

All this accounts for the controlling idea that has appeared in all the texts and rough drafts for a *continuous* education from nursery school to the university, one that respects the personality of the child then of the adolescent, and unequivocally encourages his need for expression while at the same time exposing him progressively to the diversity of artistic idioms. From this must follow proposals as to schedules, methods, and teacher training which may differ with various levels, but which will maintain a common objective varied according to the age, interests, and tastes of the individual.

For example, within the context of secondary education one can envisage replacing the traditional drawing class by a studio of expression where the supervisor of art education will be at the disposal of the students and will also propose exercises in sensitization to various means of expression; at the level of advanced classes, for those students who have chosen an art major for their

143

school-leaving certificate, he would work together with a teacher of art history, who would make every use of audio-visual aids, such as projectors, art films, etc... Students and teachers could invite artists and technicians to present their work and discuss it, as well as to lead sessions in the studio of expression or debates within the framework of a cultural club or a socio-cultural group in a *lycée*. Liaison would be established with museums, galleries, and contemporary art centers. So many dreams, some visionary, some less so, could entirely transform the existing situation in a matter of years. They have already become practical reality here and there, thanks to some enterprising departures from the old ways, unfortunately without any effect on the scene as a whole...

The training of art specialists

We have already pointed out that the training of art specialists, whether art producers, art teachers, museum curators, or teachers and scholars of art history, has been perpetuating a form of instruction that is haunted by Renaissance models from which contemporary art has made a dramatic break.[3] Even in so specialized a field as the degree course in the history of art, there is only one certificate that covers "modern times," that is to say the period from the sixteenth century to our own day; it is only their withdrawal into the past that makes cultural studies acceptable to the university, so the rare instructors who treat the twentieth century never go further than the art movements of the 1920s. One of the achievements of May and June 1968 was that it gave recognition to the autonomous existence of contemporary art as a unity of teaching and research, but without clearly considering how the question of the artistic present relates to the university.

Moreover, all these specialized forms of training have been operating up to now in isolation, without contact or collaboration with each other; they are pulled between different organizations and between different ministries. At the colloquium in Amiens a project was put forward that would involve the suppression of the existing schools and centers in favor of an all-embracing set-up, a *College or University of the Arts*. This proposal initially came from art teachers as they became aware of the handicaps that beset them; they wanted university promotion on a par with other teachers; in view of their numbers and outlook they tended to give insufficient weight to the history of art as a field for theory, research, and instruction. The revolution of May 1968 led for the first time to contacts between these different circles, resulting in a large number of projects, which varied in conception from one group or clique to another.

Without entering into the details of those discussions, let us recall the guiding principles: the main object consisted in organizing a common core of courses that would correspond to the freshman year in universities. The students, the majority of whom would be issued a school-leaving certificate in the arts, would thus benefit from a common initial training that would include the humanistic sciences (sociology, psychology, and the semiology of art) and provide a practical and theoretical grounding; after that, a large number of options would allow increasing specialization, a certain number of these options corresponding to a "unity of studies," the equivalent of a degree; changes of program would be allowed during the period of specialization, so that the student could pass from specialization in education to research or art production or vice versa. For those choosing research there would be an institute that also permitted specialization in the problems of art education.

Although future art historians would have at their disposal a studio to introduce them to techniques, there would be several studios for future art producers, allowing them to experiment in all the traditional techniques as well as with modern materials and new technological possibilities; creators and technicians of the most diverse kinds would be able to go on to a College or University of this kind in the capacity of visiting professors or "artists in residence." (The experience of American universities is worth studying in this area.) They would offer guidance in the experimental studios and organize seminars to discuss their plans, problems, and work. The teachers would play a coordinating role, thus bringing to an end the antiquated and oppressive system that has been condemned in all art schools, i.e. the system of professors who pontificate, correct, and write reports. Students and instructors would work together on collective projects, publicly and collectively criticizing these projects without regard to hierarchy or classification.

This new kind of relationship between teachers and taught may seem new in France, but its pedagogical value was proved in the successful poster studio that came into being in May 1968 after the occupation of the École des Beaux-Arts; it continues to function, and the idea has since spread to other schools. The exceptional achievement of this studio was to produce about 350 different posters, with a total printing of 600,000 copies, whose political impact was considerable. In design they were advanced by comparison with the traditional type of political poster of parties on the left; opposed by all the powerful means of mass communication, they maintained a network of independent information in constant touch with the struggle being carried on by students and workers.

Of particular significance was the innovative character of the popular studio from the pedagogical point of view, for we saw the birth of a new kind of collective, anonymous work in which professionals and students could collaborate in producing posters that arose out of a political analysis of the events and discussions outside; at the end of the day the projects were democratically proposed in the general assembly and put to the vote. They were to be judged according to two criteria: "Is the political idea sound?" and "Does the poster convey this idea well?" Thereupon the accepted projects were carried out by teams that worked in shifts around the clock, either in serigraphy or lithography. (It is worth remarking that in this way a new technique could make its appearance within art schools, namely serigraphy, which no one had previously taught.)

The stimulation of interest in art and culture

Broadly considered, the school is still the indispensable tool for eventually solving the double problem of training art producers and the public; but as a short-term policy we can now consider certain possibilities for reducing the gap between contemporary art and the masses and establishing a new relationship between them; this is one of the essential tasks in the stimulation of culture, which consists in a training in the visual arts and a development of artistic sensibility among older children and adults outside the context of school. A number of dangers await an undertaking of this kind: it may prove a futile effort in comparison with the magnitude of the problem, or it may amount to participation in the ideological enterprise of deceit whereby culture becomes a reassuring religion that completes the ideological education the bourgeoisie has received at school. Many of those who are engaged in stimulating an interest in the arts were forced by the events of May 1968 to take their bearings in relation to their social function and to ponder the possibility of operating within a revolutionary perspective.

Up to now, the arts of painting, sculpture, and architecture have no network of clubs that are comparable in importance to the ciné-clubs for the film or the Music Society for French Youth for music. A rather limited number of interested people spend weekends or attend elementary courses that are devoted to the visual arts within the framework of official organizations such as the Ministry of Youth and Sports or voluntary adult education associations like People and Culture, the Workers' Cultural Center, and the Research Group for Education and Promotion.

Here is a vast field in which valuable work could be done by educators, artists, and art students; an awareness of their social responsibilities could bring new forces into this cultural crusade and at the same time allow them to find their niche in society and the chance of status. In Havana there is a school that provides a two-year course for "art monitors" who then return to their own communities to spread art education among the masses and encourage individual expression in the arts.

We can imagine how, for instance, art students who had benefited from contact with an artist whom they had invited to come with some of his work would then show it to youth clubs, art groups, young workers' associations, business committees, etc. This kind of art diffusion would not be submerged beneath the fashionable ritual of openings as at galleries and museums, but would be the occasion for an exchange of views. The employment of the techniques of cultural stimulation does not aim at breeding passive art consumers, but at multiplying the number of active and critical participants in the adventure of art.

As for the artists, they vary in their aptitude for the human contact and verbal communication that are required of anyone who is going to stimulate an interest in the arts; this is one of the reasons why the Houses of Culture are dominated by men of the theater, for oral exchanges with the public coincide with their professional work. Nevertheless, quite a number of painters and sculptors have already undertaken such activities, especially in community cultural centers, where they direct galleries or studios, organize exhibitions, and make contact with schools. They are at present hoping to be supported in their efforts by the communities and to achieve professional status (which only exists in the staff of the Ministry of Agriculture) as well as contracts with professional guarantees.

All this presupposes a concerted policy of training specialized cultural stimulators, for whom there will be an ever-increasing need. The sociologist Joffre Dumazedier estimates that they will number 50,000 in France by 1980. This training, which could be defined as a priority among priorities, has until now been totally neglected, and this is not without its effect upon the present difficulty of effective action in the sphere of culture. Until the completion of the project for a *College or University of the Arts*, a training organization must fill the gap, whether it be a university technological institute, an interministerial center, or an institute managed by the adult education movements. It will have to be structured in a sufficiently flexible way to allow not only for the training of those who will be professionally concerned with encouraging interest in culture, but also for the inclusion of artists as probationers and associates. Moreover if an influx of failed artists into this kind of work is to be avoided, a great deal of imagination will be needed in devising schedules what will interfere as little as possible with the artists' creative work.

By contrast. the plasticians, who will receive this training and who will undertake the tasks of stimulation for varying lenths of time, will be particularly well equipped by their own work to maintain the two poles of true cultural stimulation in permanent tension: to train the greatest number in the visual languages worked out by a small group of specialists, while arousing a critical and active form of receptivity, and *simultaneously* to encourage the greatest number in visual expression.

What emerged more clearly from the events of May 1968 was the general need for *expression*, and the demand for it is totally justified if it is not naively or demagogically confused with the development of a *language*. A number of individuals showed a marked desire to express themselves by oral, written, or visual means, and at the same time many innovations took place in the forms of struggle and organization; these facts combine to reveal a "creativity" that had been socially and psychologically hindered and which was eager to make a free response to all the frustrations that had been imposed. This was particularly shown in the sphere of the visual arts by the inscriptions and the manufacture of billboards, streamers, photographic montages, etc., as also in some enterprises in which professionals and non-professionals worked as a team on frescoes, sculptures, and collective objects or in studios of "visual expression."

The aim is obviously not to multiply the number of Sunday painters, who in almost all cases are content to imitate the most reassuring pictorial models and stereotypes, such as the color-prints of the petty bourgeoisie. We no longer need to increase the number of studios or academies which parallel the school in offering an academic training with casts, life models, and still life. What requires stimulation is individual or collective expression of a more spontaneous and violent kind. If the individual is drawn is drawn into collective enthusiasm and is deeply involved, it will allow him to go beyond the limits

148

of the Sunday painter, a form of artisanlike pottering, and thereby discover, at an elementary level, some of the means of expression of the contemporary language of the visual arts.

To encourage this type of expression, which is an aspect of that "multiple anonymous germination" that Dubuffet reproaches Culture for ignoring and sterilizing, will at the same time develop a new attitude to modern art—an attitude that will no longer be one of rejection in consequence of feeling excluded or alternatively one of religious respect as for some sacred initiation. Expression in the visual arts becomes an experience which facilitates a natural approach to modern painting and sculpture; it constitutes the best of exercises in forming the sensibility.

Only naivety or demagogy would lead anyone to confuse this free expression with works produced by specialized artists who invent significant new forms that run counter to inherited forms in the course of more and more total commitment. The social consequences of the division of labor will long maintain the gulf that has widened between the specialists in art production, whether one calls them professionals or not, and individuals who experiment individually or collectively. It is certainly possible to imagine a future society of the kind evoked by the esthetician E. Fischer, in which "The artistic adventure will no longer be a privilege, but the permanent state of free and active man."` But we shall live for a long time yet with what has come to be seen as an injustice—the monopoly of the creativity of all by a minority of "experts" known as artists. Those who wish to stimulate the public in the direction of art must bear in mind both the historical conditions in which this situation has existed and also how shocking the situation is; and so they must work in two directions at the same time: they must hand on a knowledge that provides access to significant forms but is neither spontaneously nor immediately available to non-specialists, and also encourage creative expression in everyone, whatever his professional specialty may be.

We here once again encounter the demand that emerged with such force in the desire to recast the whole of art instruction; this demand is connected with the more general concern that reforms should not be to the advantage of the bourgeois class, regardless of whether the aim is the modernization of outmoded teaching that no longer corresponds to the needs of the economy, or the reinforcement of a bourgeois ideology. That is to say that art education and cultural action, which are interconnected, must not be inspired solely by a democratic and humanistic ideology that aims at reducing cultural inequalities.

149

The problem is not a simple apportioning of cultural goods or the organization of cultural leisure which would turn everyone into a passive and admiring consumer of reassuring cultural values.

On the contrary, the public must be encouraged to participate at all levels of social reality, to act in their own socio-professional sector and at the political level against the existing structures.   This is where the role of the art instructor or stimulator is of paramount importance, for he can help free the potential for confrontation in works of art, which for the most part are in opposition to the existing structures.

Thus art education, the training of art specialists, and the stimulation of cultural interest are the stakes in a constant ideological struggle; they can either integrate the artist, his works, and the public in a repressive society by acclimatizing their sensibility and behavior to an acceptance of the existing state of affairs, or else turn artists and the public into forces that are capable of fighting against the existing order on behalf of new social relationships.   In the cultural sphere that we have proposed for the visual arts, the way in which producers and the public are trained will perhaps in the years ahead undergo radical changes that will either reinforce the existing socio-cultural system or else better equip it to attack that system for its deflection of works of art from their true public and their liberating role.

August-September 1968

1. Cf. Pierre BOURDIEU, *Champ intellectuel et projet créateur* in *Temps modernes*, November 1966, Raymonde MOULIN, *Le marché de la peinture en France*, Éditions de minuit, Paris, 1967, Pierre GAUDIBERT, *Le marché de la peinture contemporaine et la crise* dans *La Pensée*, October 1965.

2. "People must be taught to see, just as they must be taught to read."   Paul Éluard.

3. In 1965 a spokesman for provincial art students protested: "The present art instuction in secondary schools is completely outmoded and useless.   It remains faithful to antiquated esthetic principles, it is false in its conception and stultifies the pupil in its application... Concepts that date from the Renaissance are held as true and taught with disarming self-assurance and a nauseating lack of curiosity.   These concepts owed their vitality to the humanism of the age, but today the sap has been cut off from them by evolution and history, and now they constitute the most desiccated and useless of academicisms."

René Micha

"The cinema rises in rebellion"
"The cinema is liberty"

The May Revolution soon hit the cinema. It couldn't have been otherwise. The cinema is a new language that borrows from the other arts and thus multiplies its abilities; it is a mirror one takes for a drive along a road, it is the art of the greatest number, and it is also, as Malraux observed, an industry and a trade. The manifestations that put an end to the Cannes Festival and disturbed those at Pesaro, Oberhausen, and Venice had one aim only—to attack the economic structure, that is to say the crying abuses of production and distribution machinery that are subject to the law of profit, the claims of the box office, the excesses of publicity, the star cult, and censorship. This is of great importance and doubtless conditions everything else, but the essential thing is still the work itself, the meaning of the work. In this respect the free assemblies, proclamations, and tracts expressed themselves in very generous terms, or not at all. It's true that the debate also covers literature, the theater, and the fine arts. And education. And, above all, society. The debate is endless.

Before coming to the questions that were put at the last International Experimental Film Competition (at Knokke-Le Zoute) and which were concerned with the significance of the film as a work of art, I should like to recall the conclusions that were reached at Paris, Cannes, and Venice—conclusions that were frequently provisional and tentative, but decisive on some points.

As we know, it all began in Paris.

Around the middle of May 1968, some young cinema technicians decided to show at the Sorbonne, Nanterre, and some lycées and factories a number of films that struck them as going "in the direction of the revolution." The École de Vaugirard became a kind of headquarters for information and political agitation. Other meetings were held at the Idhec or at the technicians' trade union center. On May 17th the scattered movements joined forces at the offices of the E.N.P.C. (National School of Photography and Cinematography) to found the States General of the French cinema. They reached agreement on the main principles, which they would strive to work out in detail in various committees; they decided on a strike to halt production and laboratory work; they called for the discontinuation of the Cannes Festival.

This Festival had already been halted for twenty-four hours. The example of Paris provoked stormy debates in which authors, critics, and organizers were attacked. Alain Resnais, Milos Forman, Richard Lester, Claude Lelouch, etc. withdrew their films. Four members of the jury resigned—Louis Malle, Roman Polanski, Monica Vitti, and Terence Young. At the moment when Carlos Saura's film *Peppermint frappé* was about to be shown, Jean-Luc Godard and François Truffaut clung to the curtain to keep it from opening. On the 18th the Festival was officially closed.

In the days and weeks that followed, the States General met at Suresnes in general assembly or in committees and worked out no less than nineteen projects designed to transform the structure of the cinema. On June 5th they tried to reach agreement on a text of composite authorship, but failed; in the end they adopted "a working basis from which every new project should evolve."

These debates were continued in Venice on the fringe of the Mostra and sometimes within it. Scenario-writers and journalists (mainly French), but also representatives of the March 22 Movement, members of the Italian left-wing political parties, and anarchists from Carrara (where another congress had just been held) tried to "create a revolution in the cinema." Here too there were interminable discussions, and the participants were not far from reaching agreement on a charter for "a cinema that is liberated from political and economic imperialisms," but they were divided as to the means and, contrary to what happened in Cannes, they didn't manage to boycott or even seriously inconvenience the Festival.

(Cannes and Venice, two more specialized Festivals, played a considerable role in the confrontation.

At Oberhausen, which was devoted to the short film, a work by Hellmuth Costard entitled *Besonders Wertvoll*, which made fun of a minister, was banned; this started a chain of demonstrations that reached as far as Parliament.

At Pesaro, where works by young authors and works that had been censored in their countries of origin were shown, there was a double split: one was between the "madmen" who entirely rejected the principle of festivals and those who considered that a festival like the one at Pesaro was in itself revolutionary and that all it therefore needed was a modification in its organization. The other split was between the revolutionaries and the police and also the neo-Fascists. More than three hundred persons were arrested, including Valentino Orsini. Urban workers soon gave their help, and screenings were able to take place, devoted that year to the Latin-American cinema. *Souvenirs d'un Pays sous-développé* by the Cuban Tomas Gutterez Alea was acclaimed.)

The excesses, inanities, contradictions, retractions, and finally the partial failure of so many efforts could not conceal the importance of what has been achieved, and it will be a lasting achievement, no matter what happens. As the *Cahiers du Cinéma* rightly said, the task in those months was to determine "the role and the responsibilities of those who conceive and make films," to consider "the problem of the function of the cinema, what alienates it as also what it alienates, what could liberate it as also what it could liberate." It seems to me extraordinary that in the course of those days and meetings, room was made for the most general views, sometimes too general, embracing too many subjects on too theoretical a plane; and yet this led to the discovery of a certain number of principles by which any genuine action will have to be inspired. The disagreements and even the contradictions—at least some of them—were perhaps not without their uses; they facilitated a greater clarity of vision.

From the start, the participants were concerned with action. The first bulletins issued by the States General declared its existence and its solidarity with workers on strike and its intention of reforming the structure of the film industry. They then ordered an unlimited strike and the occupation of buildings (these orders were hardly obeyed); they decided to found a special school for audio-visual techniques; they declared that the C.N.C. (National Council for Cinematography) had ceased to exist; they demanded that a new body replace it, covering both the cinema and television and concerning itself with both technical and artistic matters. However, toward the end of May 1968 the States General examined the new structures. Four projects were submitted to the vote of the general assembly. They differed on several points. Some differences were of the kind that tend to arise between one profession and another—the technicians were more attentive or more sensitive to questions

153

concerning their trade than were the film-writers. Other differences, as in the great days of '89, were ones of faction—severe or less severe, intransigent or less intransigent, "realistic" or less "realistic." Project 13, proposed by the delegates of the C.G.T., claimed the right to control the means of production, distribution, teaching, and research—that is to say, self-management. This can as well be brought about in a socialist economy by public means (a government sponsored credit organization) as in a liberal economy that relies on the private sector; the two sectors can coexist, they can even cooperate as well in one country as in co-productions involving another country. Project 16 came from a group of directors—Alain Resnais, Louis Malle, Jacques Doniol-Valcroze, Pierre Kast, Jacques Rivette, René Allio, Robert Lapoujade, etc. They systematically contrasted the new structures with the present stituation. They declared that today's cinema is dominated by the profit motive; in all that relates to production, choice of works, distribution, operation, and the real needs of the audience, films at all stages of the process are and remain merchandise. The C.N.C., which represents the State, serves as a shield to the system; the so-called art cinemas and experimental cinemas serve as an alibi; incontestable artistic successes only come by chance. To this must be added public and private censorship, the gaps in a cinematographic education to which few are admitted and which is cut off from a general education, the lag in techniques, and the arbitrary division that is maintained between the cinema and television. To break up this system, the authors of the project intend to make a *tabula rasa* of the existing regulations, particularly those that organize surveillance and censorship or artificial divisions. On the positive side, they propose that box-office receipts should be collected "by an organization exclusively responsible for the banking, auditing, and immediate redistribution of this money." (This is the principle from which musicians and playwrights have long benefited through the S.A.C.E.M. and the S.A.C.D.) They demanded the setting-up of a licensed public corporation that should be autonomous and free from the profit obsession. This corporation would rely on production units (in the artistic, technical, and financial senses of the word), on a promotion and distribution organization, and on publicly-owned theatres. In every case the objectives and means were described, the role of the State was defined, and the responsibilities of the permanent council of the States General and its delegates were mapped out. Project 19 was defended by Michel Cournot and a few others—Claude Lelouch, Robert Enrico, Jean-Gabriel Albicocco, Marcel Carné; it favored "creative groups," work cells for producers, authors, actors, and technicians, while its aim, function, methods, salaries, and interest in revenue recall the studios that reformers conceived in previous centuries. The films created by these groups would be distributed by a "national society for distribution" with which two other groups would closely cooperate—the "accountancy group" and the "promotion group." Project 4, which was by far the most radical, was the work of Claude Chabrol and his friends at the U.N.E.F. He wanted all shows to be free; the State should finance the entire production (thus the audience would become the producers); entry into the profession should be open to all (first stage—preliminary investigation; second stage—discussions with professionals and attendance at "film-schools"); culture should be genuinely decentralized; the production of films, professional training, and the distribution of films should be guaranteed in all regions. I shall quote from project 15, which was rejected at the final vote. It was offered by Ado Kyrou, the editor of *Positif*, and it advocated in principle that the cinema should be run by those who make it, be independent no matter what the set-up of the State, and rely on a close collaboration with the audience, who would hence also be promoters. This composite project confined itself to tacking together the texts that had apparently raised the fewest objections; it was very full, but unfortunately it ran off in every direction and revealed what Tacitus called the styles of too many hands. As for the final motion, which was voted on at the end of the States General, it went as follows:

"The States General of the cinema took their origin from a popular movement of confrontation and struggle against the existing economic, social, and ideological order, that of capitalism, which is protected by the State machine. The States General have as their objective to make cultural life and hence the cinema, which is essential to the life of the nation, a public service.

1. The destruction of monopolies, the creation of a single national organization for the distribution and operation of films, with direct collection of money in the theaters. The creation of a national organization for technical necessities —laboratories, studios, film materials, etc.

2. Self-management in order to fight against the rule of the mandarins, academicism, and bureaucracy. Officials at every rank will be elected for a limited period, supervised and subject to dismissal by those who elect them.

3. The creation of self-governing production groups that will not be subject to the capitalist law of profit.

4. Abolition of censorship.

5. The integration of audio-visual instruction into the general framework

of reorganized education; self-government by teachers and students, and free access by all social classes.

6. A close union of the cinema with a self-governing television that is independent in terms of power and money."

I have said that the echo of these great meetings, already grown so faint, would be heard again in Venice; there, side by side with some of the film-writers I have mentioned, as well as others who, like Jean Rouch, attended the sessions in Avignon, were the Italian revolutionaries, Phil Bugstein, Niko Papatakis—and Alexander Kluge (who won the *Lion d'Or*). They discussed the relationship between the cinema and politics, the possibilities of a revolutionary cinema, and the form that such a cinema should take. They considered the question of festivals, of which the least censurable was perhaps the one in Venice. They concluded with the assertion that a new cinema, whatever form it took, would always run the risk of being absorbed by organizations or the bourgeoisie. This is a bitter observation that could be read between the lines of many an article in *l'Arc* which, in connection with Jean Dubuffet and *Art brut*, pondered whether it was permissible for subversion, while borrowing from the channels of culture, to remain outside culture. But the Trojan Horse only stayed one night.

Films are called experimental when they revitalize, or try to revitalize, the language of cinematography. The last time films of this kind were entered —it was at Knokke-Le Zoute in December 1967—one clear question was raised: the role of cinema in society.

Up to that point the discussions had centered on the experimental character of the films that were presented. Of some it was said that they were of great quality but on closer consideration one found nothing genuinely original about them—they were nothing but skillful applications of earlier discoveries. In others the spirit of research could be detected, but so embryonically that one could not be sure what would one day emerge from them. The former were too perfect—one could see in them every inch of the road they had traveled; the latter were simply rough drafts, or even less, for the first idea to come along could be classed as an experiment—it was enough to wear a hat backwards. To be honest, I should add that praise sometimes went to a work whose originality seemed worthwhile enough to inspire confidence. Thus, for example (I am relying on my memory), the first International Competition (in 1949) gave awards to *Motion Painting No. 1* by Oscar Fishinger, *Fiddle-de-dee* by

Norman McLaren, *Aubervilliers* by Elie Lotar, and Kenneth Anger's first films; the second (organized in 1958, the year of the Brussels Exhibition) gave awards to *Dom* by Walerian Borowczyk and Jan Lenica, *Free Radicals* by Len Lye, *L'Opéra-Mouffe* by Agnès Varda, a short film by Roman Polanski, and the complete works of Stan Brakhage; the next (in 1963) gave awards to *Die Parallelstrasse* by Ferdinand Khittl, *Le Nez* by Alexandre Alexéieff, *Twice a Man* by Gregori Markopoulos, etc. This list shows that the prize-winning films satisfied different kinds of scrutiny; some were original in form, others in content. (Of course this distinction is an unreal one, but it is convenient, it fits in with our impressions and, allowing for due precautions, it serves its purpose.) *Free Radicals* plays a game with the eye or the mind, whereas *Aubervilliers* is a pamphlet. In some cases the division is less distinct; Agnès Varda presumably uses cut-outs to compel us to see better what strikes her as terrible or farcical, while Gregori Markopoulos modifies the usual narrative technique to evoke a myth, but clearly someone else could tell us something different by further rearranging the material.[1]

Nevertheless, the young men and women who went to Knokke-Le Zoute—and they numbered two or three thousand—were annoyed. Not all, not for the same reasons, not in the name of the same ideology. Some adhered to Moscow, others to Peking or Havana; there were also Trotzkyites and anarchists; there were trouble-makers, opportunists, and hippies, or flower children. The majority were students or ex-students. Only a small number were serious—but they counted for much; once they began to talk, it was clear that they talked sense. There were numerous prophetic pronouncements and arguments, and there were demonstrations that tended to interrupt the showing of films or create disorderly scenes; jokes were revived from Dada and *The Breasts of Tiresias*, there were happenings tinged with eroticism, and a mass passion that was always ready to leap out and pounce on its prey. Anger arose from the fact that the films seemed to have their being in a world apart, which was absolutely alien to our world and our problems; they sacrificed everything to fantasy, rhetoric, and stylistic considerations; they avoided any kind of human involvement and played interminably with forms. In a word, they gave us nothing of what we expected, what was important to us, or what we needed. Some demonstrators carried placards that said, "Down with the silent film," and they shouted for a cultural revolution that would also be iconoclastic. There can be no doubt that what arose was a great argument about formalism, but paradoxically, the occasion was an enterprise dedicated to experimentation.

157

Still from the film *Les Amours d'une Blonde* by Milos Forman

Still from the film *La Guerre est Finie* by Alain Resnais

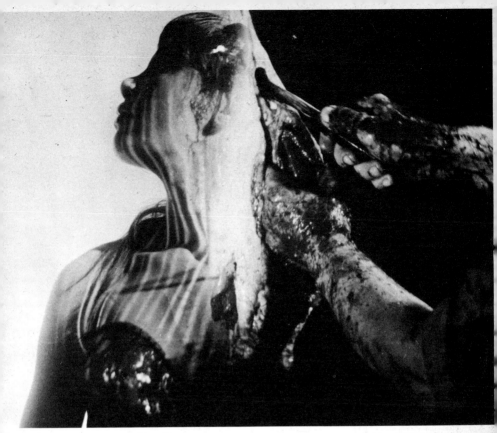

ll from the film *Herostratus* by Don Levy

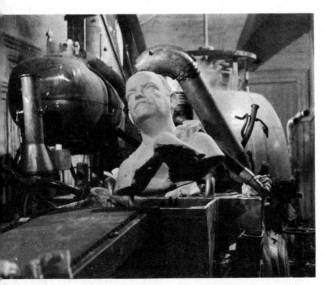

ll from the film *La Muerte de un Burocrata* by Tomas Gutierez Alea

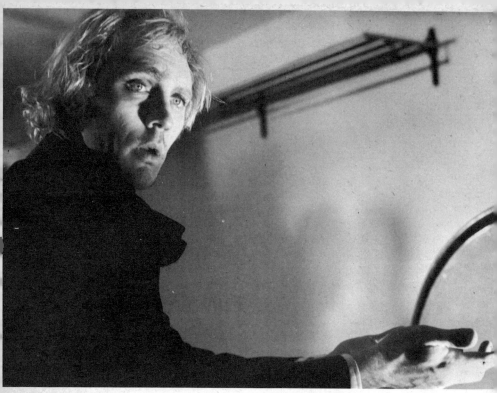

Still from the third of *Extraordinary Stories*, a film by Federico Fellini inspired by Edgar Allan Poe

Still from the film *Planet of the Apes* by Franklin J. Schaffner

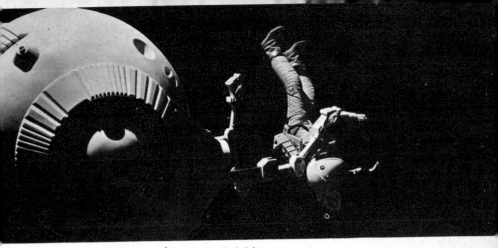

 till from the film *2001, Space Odyssey* by Stanley Kubrick

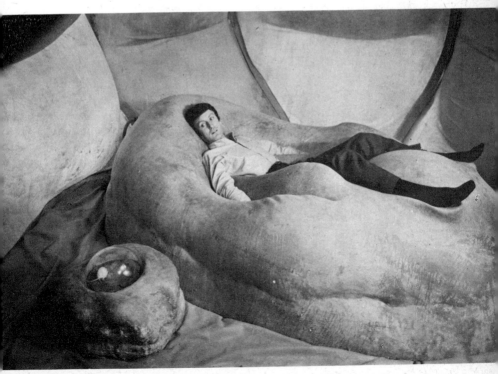

Still from the film *Je t'aime, je t'aime* by Alain Resnais

ill from the film *17th Parallel* by Joris Ivens

BOMBARDEZ HA-NOI!

ll from the film *Loin du Viêtnam*, a group work

Still from the film *Accident* by Joseph Losey

Still from the film *Petulia* by Richard Lester

Still from the film
A Propos de Quelque Chose d'Autre
by Vera Chytilova

Still from the film
Self-Obliteration by Yud Yalkut

Still from the film
Firemen's Ball by Milos Forman

Still from the film
The Bed by James Broughton

Still from the film
Wavelength by Michael Snow

Still from the film
Erlebnisse der Puppe by Franz Winzents

Still from the film
Chinese Checkers by Stephen Dwos

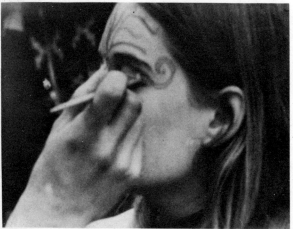

Still from the film
Peacemeal by Albert Allota

Still from the film
Portrait of Jason by Shirley Clarke

Still from the film
Josef Kilian by Pavel Juracek and Jan Schmi◀

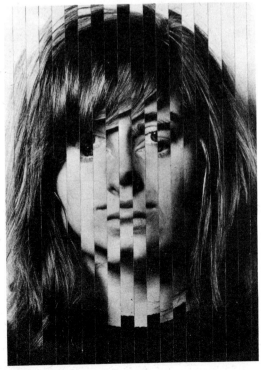

Still from the film
Schnitte by Peter Grobe

It seems to me that the rebels were partly right, but that they were right in opposition to themselves, in opposition to what they were and what society had made of them. The films that they rejected were the work of people like themselves: boys and girls in San Francisco, Berlin, London, Paris, Stockholm, Prague, Tokyo, Krakow, or Rome, who regularly pronounced themselves against misery, against black ghettos, against the war in Vietnam (several of them had gone to prison for that), but who, strangely, never dealt with these subjects in their films. There, in fact, could be seen a long waking dream, needing to push ever further the power of the object, of the machine, of the moment, of words, of festivities, and, in a real sense, insane love, a violent liberty. Why did these authors not deal with "concrete" problems, political problems, social problems? Some of those who were at Knokke explained this. They were ready to run risks for a cause that was important to them—for example, to occupy the precincts of the Pentagon or to take part in black riots—but a sort of reserve prevented them from making a film about it. A documentary perhaps, and preferably short; but they confessed to a preference for parody or simply entertainment. Besides, in their eyes, pleasure domes, L.S.D., sexual freedom, the extravagances of *pop*, speed, noise, were subjects as important as the war or racial segregation: more important perhaps, because they were the signals or the covers for alienation. They were able to say, as the *Cahiers du Cinéma* once said, that "to make a revolution in the cinema necessarily implies making it before or at the same time everywhere else"... that one has "few chances to change the cinema in an unchanging society."

The rebels were wrong, however, on other points, not merely because several of the films that were shown—in particular the admirable *Portrait of Jason* by Shirley Clarke, the terrifying *Théâtre de M. et Mme Kabal* by Walerian Borowczyk, and the superb *Herostratus* by Don Levy—moved in the direction they wanted; not merely because the organized discussions tended without exception to break down the barriers between the arts and the disciplines of the mind, to reject censorship and to establish art more firmly within society or, to borrow the title of the final discussion, to place "art in the street"—but because today's confrontation is making itself felt on all fronts, and it cannot be separated from the question of language—of the Word, as Ponge says in his *Malherbe*.

In this light, such different works as *Erlebnisse der Puppe* (the portrait of a tyrant) by Franz Winzentsen, *The Great Blondino* (existence versus Johnson) by Robert Nelson and William Wiley, *The Bed* (from birth to death) by James

Drawing from the animated cartoon *Théâtre de Monsieur et Madame Kabal* by Walerian Borowczyk

Broughton, *Chinese Checkers* by Stephen Dwoskin, *Schnitte* by Peter Grobe, *Peacemeal* by Albert Allotta and *Self Obliteration* by Jud Yalkut took on the appearance of supplies for combat or objects of scandal. As for Michael Snow's *Wavelength*, which won the *Grand Prix*, it didn't merely constitute, as people said, a technical achievement, but was a concrete expression of the relation between man and the world.

There is an unfortunate tendency for political revolutions to adapt themselves in other spheres to the most conservative mentality, even though these spheres are clearly allied to politics. And this mentality soon becomes the only one they will allow. At about that time a long article appeared in the Peking *People's Daily*, describing how a red guard painted a portrait of *Mao visiting the mines of Anyan*; it was reproduced by the million and delighted the workers, peasants, and soldiers. The painter, we were told, only relied for an instant on the 1921 photographs to recreate "the red sun that illuminates our hearts," heroism, invincibility, and glory in a setting of coal mines, mountains, and the rivers that Mao had to cross to get there (an old umbrella symbolically alludes to this), his hair blowing in the autumn wind, while the agitated folds in his long robe announce the Revolution. This young guard knew no more than the rudiments of his art, but Mao's thought guided him to the end. And so on. The stupidity of this article is disquieting, like that of the Moscow censors who suppressed dozens of pages in Mikhail Boulgakov's allegory, *The Master and Marguerite*. But returning to the subject of the cinema, we observe how the effects of reaction are the same no matter what the regime; a great machine like Bondartchouk's *War and Peace*, which constantly betrays a nostalgia for the Czarist era, with its grand figures, its balls, and even its good fellowship, is undoubtedly worse (in the most meaningful sense) than the films of the previous period which were entirely given over to socialist realism, just as *Uncle Tom's Cabin* is not as bad as more recent films like Guy Green's *A Patch of Blue*; here, as in a serial story, reappears Sidney Poitier, "the best black actor in the United States." And again: how can we accept Pier Paolo Pasolini's "poem" (published in *Epoca*), in which the director of *The Gospel according to St. Matthew* and *Teorema*,[2] who was present at the clashes in May 1968, sides with the police against the students? Because the former are workers' sons and the latter, after all, sons of the bourgeoisie? Such concepts are all the more extraordinary in that all those who were present, including Adrienne Mancia of *The Village Voice*, accused the police of incredible brutality. I read in *Esprit*: "Behind the police was the nameless target the paving-stones were aimed at; it was authoritarian conservatism, stupid bureaucracy, complacent advertising, the abstract cruelty that condemns a third of humanity of famine; it defeats our revolutions and crushes our hopes. To be sure, among these young insurgents the sons of the bourgeoisie formed the largest part. But they wanted to be—and all this time they were—something other than sons of the bourgeoisie."

On the subject of the contemporary cinema, I should like to point out:

1. That a large number of films have been made on subjects of direct interest to us. On the war in Vietnam: *17e Parallèle* by Joris Ivens, *Loin du Vietnam* by Alain Resnais, William Klein, Joris Ivens, Agnès Varda, Claude Lelouch, and Jean-Luc Godard. On the bitter fruits of the Algerian war and the Spanish Civil War: *Muriel* and *La Guerre est finie* by Alain Resnais. On racism:

170

Dutchman by Anthony Harvey. On the third world: *Terra en Trance* by Glaube Rocha. On the cultural revolution: *La Chinoise* by Jean-Luc Godard, *La Cina è vicina* by Marco Bellocchio, *Prima della Rivoluzione* by Bernardo Bertolucci. On sexual liberation: *I am curious* by Vilgot Sjöman. On psychoanalysis: *Persona, The Hour of the Wolf* by Ingmar Bergman. On arbitrary rule: *Josef Kilian* by Pavel Juracek and Jan Schmidt, *La Muerte de un Burocrata* by Tomas Gutterez Alea. On violence: *Bonnie and Clyde* by Arthur Penn, *In Cold Blood* by Richard Brooks. On sports: *Treize Jours en France* by Reichenbach and Lelouch, *Cassius le Grand* by W. Klein. On science-fiction: *Planet of the Apes* by Franklin J. Schaffner, *Je t'aime, je t'aime* by Alain Resnais, *2001, a Space Odyssey* by Stanley Kubrick. On the consumer society: *Qui êtes-vous Polly Magoo?* by W. Klein, *Blow-Up* by Michelangelo Antonioni, those of Edgar Allan Poe's stories that inspired Federico Fellini, the works of Milos Forman, *Éclairage intime* by Ivan Passer, *Accident* and *Boom* by Joseph Losey, *Le Départ* by Jerry Skolimovki, *Week-end* and other films by Jean-Luc Godard, *Play Time* by Jacques Tati, *Petulia* by Richard Lester, *A propos de quelque chose d'autre* and *Les petites Marguerites* by Vera Chytilova, *Les Gauloises bleues* by Michel Cournot, *Artisten in der Zirkuskuppel: Mastlos* by Alexander Kluge.

2. That these films—a few of the many I could have chosen— achieve their objective while following widely differing paths. They are not all equally true or effective, sometimes they keep to the path and sometimes they stray from it; sometimes they founder upon the rock of Pride, fall into the lake of Indifference, or get lost in the sea of Danger before catching sight of Revolution.

It is clear that *17ᵉ Parallèle* and *Loin du Vietnam* are about different subjects and in any case employ a different language... There are parts of *Loin du Vietnam* that many would consider feeble or useless, sacrificing seriousness of purpose to Narcissism. But I would never suggest that the work is to be condemned because of too evident exposure of technical means and esthetic inventiveness, or because it passes beyond actuality and offers thoughts and elements that are close to fiction.

At a first viewing, *Muriel* and *La Guerre est finie* appear to allow events only a minor role; they couldn't be compared to films like *Mourir à Madrid* by Frédéric Rossif or *La Bataille d'Alger* by Pontecorvo. I am, however, putting my case to those who saw them some time ago. Alain Resnais' images stay in our memory just as they stay in the momory of the characters, taking permanent possession of it, even if they are blurred, troubling it like some secret evil, making us ashamed.

A documentary has its virtues; a fictional work has others. Everybody is agreed about that, I imagine. But some people, without always admitting it aloud, would like fiction to have a more clearly established argument. They demand "positive" works, all tending thematically in the same direction. They accept nuances but they will not tolerate ambiguity or roundabout methods. Others—and these are a larger group—ceaselessly attack the excesses of formalism. If a film breaks with the traditional narrative modes, if either the sound or the image is fragmented in an unusual way, so as to bring about a new organization of time or space, they accuse it of intellectualism, estheticism, or hermetism. According to them, a revolutionary work, or simply an honest one, does not lend itself to this technique; it makes straight for the mark, it speaks a clear language that is intelligible to everyone, and its beauty immediately strikes the eye and ear.

These ideas and others of the same kind have lost authority in the last few years; but unless we stay on our guard, they may return. They have recently been heard again in France, Italy, Germany, and elsewhere. Some students have a bad conscience when the subject of conversation comes around to the people, or the workers, and they believe it is good manners (or good politics) to attack the "counter-revolutionary" tricks of the New Cinema as sheer sterility, pointless brilliance, and provocation. They willingly resort to the tactic of amalgamation —in their diatribes they confuse works which have nothing in common except that they were shown in the same theaters. Now, it is true that great confusion reigns in the cinema, and it is aggravated by screaming publicity and the bad faith of the press.

But this does not mean that the films by Fellini, Antonioni, or Lester, for example, cannot be considered as, in varying degrees, highly effective in their confrontation of some of today's social stereotypes. *Blow Up* and *Petulia* are doubtless based on narratives (one by Julio Cortazar, the other by John Haase) which aim at something else (at the kind of truth that the writer demands from the unveiling of the human heart, or from allegory), but in these cases the function of the scenario-writer is to catch in passing a wider significance, which the camera will illumine at the same time as the rest—the strange customs of the hippies, the pastimes of American children, the supermarkets open day and night (with the balloon-seller at the entrance), the performances of roller-skaters and penguins, Alcatraz, television, fashion, Market Street, or King's Road. This kind of intention could be seen even more clearly in the film that Fellini based on one of Poe's stories—one that Baudelaire did not translate. All he kept was the argument, which provides the title—*Never Bet the Devil your Head*. But he entirely invents the scenes that take place in the television studios and on the roads—I mean they do not follow Poe.

I am very fond of Milos Forman's films—*L'As de Pique, Les Amours d'une Blonde, Au Feu les Pompiers*. These films photograph what they see, or at least they arrange men and things so felicitously that they give that impression (although the director is doubtless infinitely more subtle and skillful than one realizes). But I am no less fond of such extremely elaborate and ornate works as *Space Odyssey*, which is less like Cyrano de Bergerac's *L'Histoire de la Lune et du Soleil* than Swift's *Treatise on Games* and Diderot's *Lettre sur les Aveugles*; I am no less fond of *Planet of the Apes*, which is *L'Ingénu* of our age, and *Je t'aime, je t'aime*, an epic poem which is comparable to those of the Middle Ages—*Huon* or *Le Chevalier du Cygne*.

The States General of the French cinema have done a good job. If they failed to demolish the building they attacked, they have shaken the foundations and the walls. Moreover, they have sketched some of the constructions that are to come—not always alike, but identical in aim. They are concerned with giving the cinema its true abode and making it habitable for all.

Discussions have centered on a popular cinema and its responsibilities to culture; no details have been spelled out. We must remember, however, that in May and June 1968, students and workers undertook to make films in the very places they occupied; in most cases they were pieces of evidence, leaves of a diary.

We must try to determine the significance of what is created. To my mind, there is no better model than the one we were given by the Soviet school of 1925. Eisenstein, Poudovkine, Koulechov, Dziga-Vertov, and Dovjenko led the revolution on several planes at once. They treated what was being achieved, what lay behind it, and what was to come; they bore witness to all the forms of man's alienation and not merely, as is sometimes said, his economic alienation; they bore witness to the contradictions of history, which makes men, but which men make. But they also transformed the language of the cinema. By their teaching and their works they created an example of montage which

173

is perfect in that it comprises all the rules and all the freedoms. In several ways the writings of Eisenstein remind one of Leonardo da Vinci's *Notebooks*. Orson Welles, Robert Bresson, Federico Fellini, and Alain Resnais are clearly his heirs. I am mingling classical and baroque names. They excite us by a rendering that sometimes adds to an event and sometimes subtracts from it. However, as in *Hiroshima*, *Giulietta degli Spiriti*, *Mouchette*, and *The Magnificent Ambersons*, the cruelty depends on the style. I would say the same of Borowczyk's *Théâtre*, which he enlivens with colored figures.

It is not easy to apply oneself to truth or poetry. "One must love the arts," wrote Henri Beyle, "one must love and be unhappy."

1. This would come with Godard, Lester, Cournot, etc.
2. Incidentally, *Teorema* is an excellent illustration of the contradictions within our society. It is a "visitation"; a young man, who seems to have borrowed his traits from Christ, seduces (in the strongest sense of the word) an entire family. The film was awarded the First Prize by the O.C.I.C. (International Catholic Office for the Cinema); but it was seized by the courts and aroused the indignation of *Osservatore Romano*.

"The cinema rises in revolt" appeared on the placards of the States General of the French cinema in May 1968. It is also the title of a publication of the States General, edited by the *Terrain Vague*, of which only one number has so far appeared. "The cinema is liberty" is the title of a manifesto by a group of revolutionaries.

Alain Jouffroy

What's to be done about art?

From the abolition of art to revolutionary individualism

to Jean-Pierre Faye and
to Jean-Luc Godard

The world does not revolve around those who invent new upheavals but around those who invent new values; it revolves *in silence*.

Nietzsche.

"The most important problem in politics is to find a means of preventing those who have no part in government from becoming the prey of those who govern them."[1]   For the man who writes, and considers his writings as instruments of action and orientation and not as an individual or social "product," the discovery and publicizing of this *means* are "the most important problem in politics."   The French materialists of the eighteenth century, who have been and still are underestimated, while the influence of their thought stretches beyond Marat and de Sade to nineteenth-century dialectical materialism, have only half-opened that door, and even today this fact is still condemned on all sides.   We now know that there are practical means of preventing the State and its subordinate institutional authorities from invariably triumphing over all opposition, every action undertaken against their will.   We have just discovered —in May 1968—that an unacknowledged void separates the system that governs us from the life and from the power of each of us.   Hovering over everything, with its money, armored cars, police, and bureaucracy, the State which all but tumbled in May is not extinguished, but it was shaken by the massive "irruption" of the forces of confrontation that demonstrated the possibility of overthrowing the archaic structure of our society, and it has since begun to "wither."[2]   And yet it behaves as though it were still merged with the complex of interests of all the nation's producers, while rationalizing as much as it can

175

the functioning of the means of production; it maintains the myth of its authority by strategically filling in all the breaches made by the revolutionaries in the institutional organization of culture, and the fate of the officials hangs on whether they manage to help perfect and reinforce this system. In fact, the State merges with nothing except its financial and bureaucratic power, and we would only be acquiescing in its self-delusion if we ascribed to it a permanent, collective reality which it does not have. The intellectual producers are those who work for the radical transformation of the ideology, a theoretical, semantic, and conceptual transformation without which the language of the future revolution would damage the very precision and effectiveness of its tactics and strategy; hence these intellectual producers have become the artisans of change, the engineers of the possible. If they renounce this task, the technocratic ideology of power will succeed without very much difficulty in imposing itself on the majority as the only "realistic" concept capable of rallying all shades of parliamentary opinion, from the extreme left to the extreme right. The very severe setback of last June must therefore serve us to perfect, clarify, and put into practice the new ideas that are opposed to the bureaucratic centralization of power and the vertical hierarchy of all values.

In the particular theoretical perspective in which I have placed myself since the "Anti-Trial" of 1960, when I joined with some fifty painters and writers in attacking the State's authoritarian morality and justice, I have made my marginal contribution as a writer to the common front of anti-imperialist intellectuals; I have also systematized my ideas in "The Objectors," "The Abolition of Art," and "Actualism," and I have been induced to define myself in relation to a revolutionary individualism whose urgency and novelty reflect the specific contradictions of the revolutionary struggle in all the industrial countries that have not yet had their revolution or in which the revolution has been sabotaged. I have thus begun to question the most widely held cultural ideas and values—the expression, the structure, and art itself (the official culture). The revolution in outlook that I have been speaking of for the last eight years would tend to transfer the power of the "artist creator" for the benefit of the viewers; this is the mental revolution which Marcel Duchamp and the orientation of several painters, poets, and scenario-writers have helped me to make clearer and more decisive than the "originality" of the works as such, and the time has now come to put the practical consequences of this into effect. I am convinced that by a change of language, by refusing to play the game of cultural normality, we shall change ourselves and shall soon come to find the methods of organization and combat that are necessary for the propagation of revolutionary ideas in the areas where they can have a genuine impact.

All the superstructures can be destroyed; no police or army will ever be able to protect them against a concerted revolutionary movement which will attack the point where ideology and power meet. By attacking the weakest point of this power—its ideology—one can explode the myth of its "inevitable necessity." The May revolution was only the prelude to a Copernican revolution in society, which will change the vertical organization of industrial and cultural production into a horizontal organization; the new viewer doesn't perceive "beauty" as the crown of a world of ugliness, truth as the peak of an awareness that begins at the bottom in error, or perfection as a goal toward which the first steps are stumbling and hesitant; he embraces the entirety of contradictions as a movement and a struggle which are unable in any way to reach completion anywhere. The danger that is permanently represented by the existence of the State over and above the lives of all men is the same danger that everyone runs on account of an ideology of base and summit, the ideology of fixed rules, and a hierarchical order which admits innovations only insofar as they do not affect these rules and this hierarchy. This danger spells death to all true creation, because it condemns men to adapt themselves to the world by strangling their liberty and silencing their true opinions.

If we continue in such a way that nothing essential can be changed in the rules of the social game, if we constantly yield before authorities that determine from above the orientation of our work and the economic conditions of production and consumption, if we resign ourselves to relinquishing the unknown part of ourselves to the State's rationalistic desire for cuts and planning, never will a social revolution, whether violent or not, be able to begin the process of really changing our lives. Man will always be the ox that ploughs the furrow of limited, monotonous, heavy work. But if on the other hand we take stock of the fact that we are all producers, and that it is on us and us alone that the meaning and purpose of all that we produce depends, that the part we play is indispensable, that our responsibility is limitless, that we can always do *more* or *something else* than we are doing, that there is no law we cannot break, that repressive force is the simple translation of collective renunciation, and that a general strike throughout the world could be launched following a new Vietnam with which everyone by a chain reaction or through telepathy could feel he was concerned, then "art" will perform the function of giving visible form to the new possibilities that are offered us, and the utopia that presides over art will finally become the most immediate and effective propaganda for a truth that will conquer and change the error of impotence into the calm certainty of again taking history into our hands. But this new awareness can only be achieved to the extent that we can re-invent all cultural values, re-see and even re-make our past by no longer obeying the historical quirks that arise from a feeling of inevitability. The primary function of the "abolition of art" is to destroy all the cultural mythologies whereby the powers-that-be crystallize the image of their own superiority, their own intelligence; art is the armchair in which the State sits for its own pleasure. There are always libraries behind heads of state; their furniture and homes reflect the power they wish to exercise over whatever opposes them. Now, we shall only change the political horizon by ceasing to revolve around an authoritarian center, we shall only come to sovereignty by refusing to delegate it to anyone at all and by living it with all our might and in all our actions. Nothing can stand against this necessity for a radical, total transformation of all the values of our culture. Thought can achieve everything—a constitution, a manifesto, a gospel, a civil code, or a new equation for the universe. It can also undo everything by imposing a truth that is universally evident.

Through this breach sprang the theoretical and practical invention of the pre-revolutionary movement in May 1968, and we saw the reality of the void that separates the State from the liberty that is discernible in the territory over which its power extends. It is in this void, which is the very air we breathe in the streets, that we can invent the counter-institutions we need if we are to control what we have been dispossessed of. A multiform and multicellular counter-state can oppose the mechanical decisions of any bureaucracy. But to open the way that leads to this counter-state, we must utilize all the most modern means of communication and introduce the simplest of apparent changes in direction and orientation. All producers must be persuaded that they must of necessity control their own means of information. If "artists"—producers of images and forms—and writers—producers of ideas—and scenario-writers—producers of audio-visual messages—really unite with all the other producers to hasten the putting into operation of a new system of communication, the State will gradually die of its own accord, for it will lose the authority of a knowledge which it no longer monopolizes. The world student revolution has no other aim than that.

One must know how to dare "to be able to be the first to put, penetrate, and resolve every question... of a general kind"; this is the principle that Lenin applied in *What's to be done?* to the necessity of making clear and emphasizing the "general domocratic tasks that confront all people." It seems to me that sixty-six years later it applies to all the needs for transformation which are now the motivating force behind the worldwide confrontation which the revolution of May 1968 initiated before the eyes of all. Just as (according to Lenin) "political class consciousness can only come from the outside, that is to say from outside the economic struggle and the sphere of relationships between workers and owners," so today, sixty-six years later, revolutionary consciousness can only come from outside each class by overturning the moral, economic, and political partitioning that works in favor of the new capitalist or pseudo-socialist autocracies. The explosion in May 1968 was far too spontaneous and too little exploited for it to avoid leading to dissatisfaction for some time after its failure, and even to the politics of despair which are extremely dangerous for revolution; but thanks to those events we have clearly learned that it is essential as a first step to invent a new method of political combat that will allow us to penetrate all classes of the population, and to that end we must organize a revolutionary reappraisal of our society in all its sectors and with the widest possible scope. The bourgeois distinction between "intellectuals" and "workers"—which Lenin was already saying in 1901 must be "absolutely obliterated"—has become, like many other distinctions of this kind, an anachronistic obstacle to that penetration of all classes and to that organization of a complete reappraisal of industrial societies.

Last year, when I wrote *The Abolition of Art*, I did not expect that seven months later the streets, universities, and areas around the factories of Paris would provide so precise, so massive a confirmation of my thesis on "cultural guerrilla warfare"; I had surprised and shocked most of the members of the French delegation at the last Cultural Congress in Havana in January 1968 by what I said on this subject in the Cuban magazine *Juventud Rebelde*. I did no more than expand on the political side of what I had said in *The Abolition of Art*, with special allusion to the struggle of producers of works of art in Europe. There is something staggering and provocative about the arguments that tend to show the political links which are formed, broken, and then more powerfully re-formed between revolutionary theory and its practical application. For most "artists" themselves, "art"—and this is the crux of the problem—is at the edge of an eternal respite, where it is inconvenient, suspect, or even blameworthy to inscribe annotations of a tactical or strategic kind. Now, it is quite clear that the difference between *The Abolition of Art* and all the previous attempts at ideological destruction (Dada in particular) is that I consciously and deliberately allied the elimination of esthetic values to the necessity and possibility of social revolution. I was not trying to add a supplementary novelty to the catalog of novelties and fashions; the abolition of art must add the final theoretical and *practical* point to fifty years of challenging traditional values, which still exist in the eyes of those concerned with their survival and in those contemporary works which are apparently most opposed to their perpetuation. It has thus become absolutely necessary on the eve of further struggles to draw the first conclusions and eliminate *for the first time* the mental block created by the depressive obsession with the "death" of the work of art, which corresponds on the political plane to the death of the idea of an infallible "scientific" dogma. The "death" of the work of art, like that of God, is a piece of *luck*—it opens up all the possibilities whereby we may free ourselves from the obsession of divisive specialization. We must now view and interpret works of art in terms of this liberating will so that as soon as the label that classifies them as art has been torn off, their real significance has a chance of making itself known to us. The *action* of thought replaces the *expression* of thought, and powerful communication is finally substituted for the mirrorlike contemplation of two desires and two disguised incomprehensions. We can now begin to discuss real things—objects, forms, intentions, and influences. But we no longer need justify them or explain them with the aid of arguments drawn from the history of art, since only their *actual* action and meaning can interest us and enlighten us. Thus most "works of art" that are still favored by the galleries of the entire world topple into the grave of dead ideas, even if they are the dead ideas of very lively old men who insist on trying to rule us to the end. This grave has bēen called an "imaginary museum," and this is certainly no accident, for what we are concerned with is the coffin that one of these living corpses has constructed in his own mind and in which he has sealed himself for the last twenty years, repeating the funeral oration and rites of all the *values* he claims to want to defend, *values* that only the State's police and army can *really* protect against all confrontation, even if it be verbal. This "death" of the work of art signifies the death of the ideology of *moral*,

180

esthetic, and *mercantile* "values." This death has enabled our thoughts—our actions will come later—to penetrate a vital area, a "true life" and not a false death, where the conflict itself—revolutionary violence is not a *value*, an end in itself, but a *means*—will be led by those who believe that the relations between man and man and the relation of thought to reality must be reshaped from A to Z. But we shall only begin to see and really grasp the "death" of the work of art as a piece of good fortune insofar as we are able, first, to make yesterday's "art" something other than an object of speculation and conservation; secondly, to invent other forms of communication than those that until now have been utilized in the commercial circuit of the "arts," of written, visual, and aural language; and thirdly, to contact and regroup the men who are available for this work—and let no one tell us that there aren't any; "men are lacking when men are in a mass."

Let us have no illusions about it: most "art critics" are going to carry on as if art were not abolished, as if art couldn't be abolished; most "artists" are going to continue to believe in the "artistic" character of their production; most gallery-goers, art lovers and, of course, buyers are going to *ignore* the fact that the abolition of art can really occur in the actual time and space of a pre-revolutionary situation like that of May 1968. It is essential that the minority advocate the necessity of going on an *active art strike*, using the "machines" of the culture industry so that we can more effectively set it in *total* contradiction with itself. The intention is not to end the rule of production, but to change the most adventurous part of "artistic" production into the production of revolutionary ideas, forms, and techniques. Thus it is not a question of "revolting" against the art and artists of the immediate past—that would be a waste of time and energy—but, as I have said, of imagining something that could penetrate all social classes and organizing a total, creative reappraisal of our society. The revolution no longer has any frontiers; it must be thought out, it must be prepared *everywhere*—in all the sectors where man expends passion and energy to do what he does, else it will *never* triumph *anywhere*.

To triumph everywhere, it is not necessary to wait for a "spontaneous" movement analogous to that of May 1968. This time it would be criminal not to prepare the way by creating centers for the formation and diffusion of revolutionary ideas. The "unpublishable" texts that I was speaking of last year must be written and semi-clandestinely published; films that have no commercial

Olivier Mosset, French, 1947-
Untitled, 1967

potential must be made, and places must be found where they can be shown. The question of collaboration with publishers and producers, etc., can no longer be considered in precisely the same terms, for we now know that the possibility exists of appealing to men from very diverse walks of life—workers, intellectuals, supervisors, technicians, etc., and especially those who understand that the dissatisfaction and anguish created by the social situation cannot be reduced to purely economic terms, but necessitate a revolution in the structure of social, hierarchical, compartmentalized, and authoritarian relationships that we have with one another. The minorities who made the May revolution knew how to expose the repressive apparatus of this society and could only make a beginning in the task of working out what must be done to liberate each one from his isolation, to bring together the separate producers and to have a revolutionary and simutaneous impact on all sectors of production. Moreover intellectuals or revolutionary "artists" must be able to count *effectively* on each other to organize a network for issuing and distributing texts and a network for making and distributing films. The material difficulties that this entails must not be taken as inherent impossibilities; now is the time when utopia can begin to take root, and semi-legal or illegal literature, like illegal cinema, will become more powerful weapons as their opposition to the existing literary and cinematographic order becomes more concrete and more political.

Only painting is in danger of remaining marginal, for it seems difficult to conceive of an "illegal" painting, unless painters devote themselves exclusively to the collective production of revolutionary posters of the same type as those created in May and June 1968 at the Popular Studio of the École des Beaux-Arts. Olivier Mosset's paintings are among the few that resist the students' desire for confrontation and the questioning of all values, and they do so because they have systematically been reduced to zero and because they show a total absence of taste. After Daniel Pommereulle, Mosset is one of the very rare painters who have put into practice the more or less conscious idea of abolishing "art." Furthermore, the series of pictures that Erró devoted to the double theme of Chinese revolutionary posters and the decoration and furnishings of American apartments is an exceptional example of communication, for without commentary it contrasts the "armed struggle" of the Vietcong with the stupefying mediocrity of the "comfort" dreamed of by the middle classes in a consumer society. The union of ideas and pictorial invention instantly takes on a political reality

Erro (Gundmundur Gundmundsson), Icelandic, 1932-
American Interior No. 1, 1968. Hercules Collection, Belville, London

Erro (Gundmundur Gundmundsson), Icelandic, 1932-
American Interior No. 5, 1968

Erro (Gundmundur Gundmundsson), Icelandic, 1932-
American Interior No. 7, 1968

Erro (Gundmundur Gundmundsson), Icelandic, 1932-
American Interior No. 9, 1968

which has never been visually represented. Here too, no "taste" intervenes to mask or blur the open meaning of the image. It no longer needs an interpretation that is founded in the traditional Manichean morality, for the infiltration by the Vietcong into the kitchens, bathrooms, and living rooms of the American petty bourgeoisie is the symbolic equivalent of the stunning entry of revolutionary ideas into all social strata. To be sure, it depicts a dreamed action, but it is also an action that the revolutionary by his own labor can turn into reality. It is said that the Vietcong fight for each one of us, but each of the revolutionary ideas, even those that are farthest removed from the war, are linked with this fight. "We must dream!" wrote Lenin at the end of *What's to be done?* and added, "I write these words, and suddenly I'm afraid." We are all there, in France and elsewhere, dreaming of a clandestine revolutionary organization capable of gradually provoking a general political awareness; faced with this situation, the enemy in power is going to make use of all possible means to deflect it from its goal, and submerge it beneath inanities, demagogy, and fear. The propaganda of bourgeois ideology is, whatever one may say, always the most powerful, for it reaches inside the minds of the revolutionaries and dissuades them from sending the signals without which we shall never be able to coordinate our actions. We are daily subject to the debilitating effects of discouragement and the contagious idea that "nothing can be done," that "the people aren't ready," that "the crowd doesn't follow," that "the intellectuals are isolated from the masses," that "the workers don't want a revolution" but only a greater share of the profits. Since May 1968 we have known that this intoxication can be fought, that it may even give up the struggle against the counter-intoxication of a revolutionary movement that is followed by the entire body of those who work.

We can only claim a position in the vanguard of this movement insofar as we truly accomplish vanguard actions and insofar as our very ideas advance beyond all analysis, beyond all previous battle tactics. The revolution is still for from being a certainty, the movement may unforeseeably lose momentum, but its chances will be greater if we are not afraid of self-criticism, not only each time we suffer a setback and each time we don't achieve our objective, as is still the case, but also each time we advance a little. Revolutionary intellectuals must therefore decide on an ideological program that will boldly indicate the originality of the pre-revolutionary situation with which we are familiar in consumer societies, in which the governments can only rely more and more on their police and their army to protect and increase the profits of shareholders and exploiters. The bourgeoisie makes little concessions to the proletariat, one by one, to persuade it of the justice of the theory of a transition to socialism that is "slow" (oh, so slow!), "peaceful" (in spite of world wars and some savagely suppressed riots), and "democratic" (in spite of *coups*). This is the situation in which the revolutionary vanguard, which has always been a minority, even in a country where it has triumphed, must redefine itself in redefining all its modes of action and subversive propaganda. I can only contribute to this if I refuse to rest content with my role of prophet and become the organizer of my own telepathy, if I can abandon the subjective methods of the solitary sniper who skirmishes with the constituted authorities and the police, and if I can lend my own passion to a new program, presenting truly new ideas that can oppose the ideas and "values" of the State and its economic and cultural myrmidons. Like each one of us, I must be prepared for an action that will stretch far beyond the too-narrow frame of literature and art, an action in which the ideas will always be more disturbing than things, the deeds of daily life will always be more immediately graspable than the works of art and literature, even if I am persuaded that the books, pictures, and films that interest us—even supposing we can release them from the traditional confines of their manufacture and sale—can become weapons of ever-increasing range. And in this battle, the only crime, according to the State and its officials, will be that of having an opinion that damages their prestige and interests. We shall only be able to make these weapons if we unite *outside* the art market, *outside* the governmental and commercial forms of culture, that is to say organize ourselves in such a way that each will be able to devote all his time to revolutionary activity without sacrificing any of his time and energy in "remunerative" activities. There will be no need for us to "make a profit," to turn ourselves into businessmen in the production of revolutionary works of art, but we must progressively develop, using all the money we can obtain to make and distribute new books and films which will establish a network of information, criticism, and true creativity; and at the same time we shall avoid the risk that mental activity may participate in the "cultural" life of the nation as at present regulated by institutions, and be finally reduced to a form of social oppression and police control. On this network will depend the chance of a real transformation in the relation between thought and thought, so that each of us may become the mental liberator, no longer the mental oppressor, of the other, because each will be able to run the risk of being in advance of himself.

At the beginning of the May revolution, Chris Marker had the idea of having 16mm "film-tracts" anonymously shot by directors, writers, photographers, and students, each lasting two and a half minutes. His initiative offered us the simplest, most original model so far of what can be done freely and autonomously by means of cinematographic writing and images. Each 16mm reel, if used as a notebook that can be filled page after page without the possibility of correction, allows a film to be shot (with the help of a single cameraman) in such a way that literally any scene of vital interest can be presented, denounced, commented upon, and interpreted in accordance with aims that are incompatible with "normal" production as conceived by the film industry and censorship. "Film-tracts" may be political documents or poems, whereby anyone can send messages to all those from whom he is quite separated by the absence of organization. The necessity of ensuring that these films are seen—there are already more than forty of them—imposes on us the task of creating a distribution network that is parallel and *opposed* to the one that already exists. At the working committee of the Writers' Union, which was founded at the time when the Hôtel de Massa was occupied, on May 21, 1968, I proposed the production of "book-tracts" to be printed in unlimited editions on offset machines; these would allow writers freedom, when they wished it, from the norms and obligations of cultural production. This system would allow an unfettered circulation of their more personal messages; and an independent literary form, enabling the author to totally disregard the taste and criteria of literary criticism in general, could arise from this new kind of book. It seems that a tradition of such publication already exists in Soviet universities, and this could be perfected or complemented by the reproduction of photographs or drawings without greatly increasing their necessarily very low price. This would be a means whereby the literary avant-garde could escape from the clans, parties, and intrigues created by the publishing cliques; it would be in direct contact with the men it wanted to win over first, men whom the present system generally alienates, leaving them in a state of indifference or disgust. Telepathy is essential if revolutionary ideas are to have immediate fascination; it is the most complete form of powerful communication, and its effectiveness would be all the more dynamic in that no jamming or distortion of its signals could be engineered by those who have long betrayed the truth, always more complex because always semi-secret, of the avant-garde's literary production. The jamming and distortion in magazines and reviews are continuous, for in the interest of sales they are condemned to discuss only the books that "sell," those issued by the "great publishing houses." The project I have proposed would for once enable the reader himself to be the first critic, the first accomplice of the object that he has been given to read, the first who is responsible for the choice he has made in buying it, and as a conscientious reader he is the equal of the man who conscientiously writes. That is to say that this very article, "What's to be done about art?" must provide the reader with an answer. I do not feel too far removed, as I did during the first fifteen years of my life as a writer, from all those for whom I write and who can give meaning to my life. I maintain that what I have said about revolutionary individualism is not incompatible with the practical necessity of organization with which we are concerned today. The most individualistic of individuals, the one who is utterly opposed to any regulation of his thought within a preestablished ideological framework, the one who believes in the subversion of individual thought when it breaks with his last solipsist illusions, the one who wishes to stamp each of his ideas, each of his actions with the characteristic and significant seal of difference, this individual who has always been considered as the potential or real enemy of any collective revolution is on the contrary *the indispensable key to such a revolution.* You won't change the world or life by herding sheep, and revolutionaries will always be distinguished from sheep in that they will make decisions and take risks *before* everyone else. The word "avant-garde" has no other meaning than that. If, like everyone in the West, I write in the midst of bourgeois society, it is under the double pressure of my own thought, which never ceases to drive me onward beyond my own convictions, and a non-"humanist" revolutionary ideology that refuses to separate the social from the individual, the economic from the political, work from leisure, and reality from utopia[3]—which is to say that I have no intention of considering my "fantasies" and my "utopia" as the fruit of the mere "originality" of individual thought. Jean Dubuffet expounds in *Asphyxiante Culture*, the most pertinent of his writings, certain ideas in *L'Abolition de l'Art*, and he prophesies, for example, that "art will no longer have a name; the notion of art will undergo a revolution, and not by art, which from no longer being named will live healthily again"; he proposes sending those "intellectuals who claim to be revolutionary" into "institutes for deculturalization, nihilistic gymnasiums as it were, where particularly lucid instructors would give a course in deconditioning and demystification lasting several years in such a way as to equip the nation with a thoroughly trained body of negationists who will keep confrontation alive, at least in small, exceptional isolated circles, amid the general

Section of *The kings of imperialism have transformed technological progress and sexuality into instruments of repression*, a "film-tract" by Chris Marker

MENSUEL - N. 2 | 2 F
BELGIQUE 20 FB - ALGERIE 2,30 DA
SUISSE 2 FS - MAROC 2,30 DM - CANADA 50 CTS

KWAÏ

POUR ADULTES

la sensibilité et

en instrument

entrenchment of cultural conformity"; in fact he wants revolutionary intellectuals to "stop being intellectuals."[4] The truth is that every individual must stop merely being what he is and become still more individual and still more revolutionary, Jean Dubuffet being one of the first. To anticipate the accusation that is liable to be made against all those who intend to maintain their right to think for themselves, each of us must revolutionize himself and achieve by his own means the maximum of freedom and distance with regard to all he has been and all that he has been able or unable to do; and first of all he must stop wanting to be or believing himself to be a "leader." But whoever thinks for himself will always be suspected of merely wanting to pursue his own interests so as to attain maximum personal prestige. It is the paradox of the revolutionary individual that he is freer and more independent than the others and is better able to denounce the lack of freedom and independence from which they suffer. Moreover I have never claimed that revolutionary individualism was anything other than a means whereby the individual may cease to be only what he is; every worker, peasant, and technician aspires to become much more than a worker, a peasant, or a technician. The intellectuals who are believed to have gained most from their "culture" are now the first to denounce its illusions and misdeeds; they will cease to be merely intellectuals insofar as they can put into practice that revolutionary individualism of which I have been speaking, which consists in the first place of inventing forms of thought and communication that can lead to an upheaval in the power structure of the hierarchical societies in which we all live. They will do so to the extent that they overcome a comfortable heritage of rebellious but non-revolutionary individualism that justifies political apathy: "one form of government is like another," "there will always be police," etc... It's not easy to see, smell, and hear what is going on under our noses and freely interpret it without taking into account the interpretations that have already been made. We can only truly advance by breaking and rebreaking the iron collar that we invent to justify ourselves and by refraining from ceaselessly turning back to all we have learned or acquired. Just as "art" is the first thing an artist must forget, so also the revolutionary individual must erase the image he has made of himself. No one can seriously claim any longer that he expresses nothing but his own thought, that "subjectivity" is the only authentic source for the "creator," that "personality" is an end in itself and an intrinsic "value," etc. Each of us brings into existence all that others are for him; his liberty is only due to their liberty, and his true thought is the telepathic current that passes simultaneously through all brains that think for themselves, in the spark of each moment that is *stolen* from non-thought. To "organize revelations for the sake of the entire population," one must begin with those who will be able most directly to contact this "population," then put oneself at the disposal of those who write and "enable to see" and shed an all-pervading light on the signals of the revelations to be made, discussed, and acted upon in terms of the *political* efficiency and orginality of these signals; to conceive and apply a language that coincides with a situation in its totality though it is only lived fragmentarily. In this work of organization, individual thought cannot be considered obstinately antagonistic since it the originating movement that brings about inventions and initiatives.

The great joy that we experienced for the first time in the streets of Paris during May 1968, that joy in the eyes and on the lips of all those who for the first time were talking to each other, although complete strangers, this was exactly the joy that the individual lacks most, for he is a prisoner of his "private life"; his function and his specialty always demand his renunciation of joy—the joy of entwining separate strands, the joy of making a *collage* of disparate situations, the joy of discovering differences, the joy of linking up solitudes, without for an instant losing the subtlest and most abstract movements of thought. Revolutionary individualism, which was no more than a theory or an intention until May 1968, has become the practical philosophy of subversive action in our society from the moment when we discovered friends and allies through the chance movement of the crowd, under the open windows, and realized that the apparently foolish idea of a violent revolution in a consumer society was there, inscribed and hung in the air like a piece of collective evidence—so surprising, so unexpected that we all became aware of having made practically no preparations for mastering it or for directing it toward more concrete achievements. Paris was cut in two by the State Police, but none of us had ever felt so full, so serene, so open, and so free. Art and literature no longer needed publishers, museums, galleries, or Houses or Ministries of Culture to "function"; everyone's thought reverberated on every wall and expressed itself on every tongue; the irrational was no longer the enemy of the rational, disproportion created its own proportion, and yet we knew that, empty-handed, we couldn't crush the police and the army with paving-stones, we knew that the only way of triumphing was to convince the waverers of their error and the necessity of correcting it with all speed; consequently we needed not merely one

Iskra, one Spark, but a hundred, a thousand *Iskras* that were suitable for all the working classes, for all the technicians, for all the supervisory personnel, and for all the marginal elements of our society. The advantage of a multiple power invented by the revolutionaries over a central power entirely controlled by the State would have allowed the French to create the first revolutionary industrial society of the twentieth century and to define the primary objectives of a revolution that was finally rid of its nineteenth-century myths, clichés, catechism, and code.

What must be done about art after this abortive fourth revolution? What must be done about literature, painting, and the cinema after the abolition of the traditional and police-controlled idea of "culture" and "art"? What must be done about the signs and symbols after this change of vocabulary and grammar? "To become a political force in the eyes of the public, it is not enough to stick the label 'avant-garde' on a reactionary theory and practice; we must work hard and obstinately to *raise* our level of awareness, our spirit of initiative, and our energy."[5] But neither is it enough to make this sentence, which Lenin wrote sixty-six years ago, the watchword for tomorrow. It is not enough to believe and wish oneself "evolutionary." It is not enough to abolish the ideas that have been corrupted by the State we want to destroy. It is not enough to wish for or even to establish the program for a revolutionary "party" or "movement." It is not even enough to change oneself and do everything in one's power to change others. Nothing is enough, not even the fact of becoming a "political force" in the eyes of the "public." We haven't done all we can to avoid being where we are, in a desert where everyone meditates by himself while looking at the flames that devour the ruins of a revolution which once again has just died and which will come to life again in another form. We haven't done all we could because we haven't been able to leap the ditch that an unforeseen situation had dug between the political inertia of a people anesthetized by the power of the State and the initiatives of the revolutionaries who occupied their colleges and factories. The institutions and institutionalized ideas resisted the spontaneous explosion. It is these institutionalized ideas that must be destroyed, and first of all they must be destroyed in ourselves. The abolition of art means the end of the nineteenth century, the end of the ideology of *values,* the end of rebellious, ironic romanticism, the end of a slow-motion History that concerns us only if it is remote. We are dead to our

200

past, dead to our old thought, dead to our old feelings.   The distance between the abolition of art and revolutionary individualism is the desert that must be crossed.   And yet we are alive, we are going to rediscover everything in obscurity, we are going to re-learn everything in ignorance.   But we must finally decide that we can no longer *re*-begin everything.   We must escape from the cycle and laws of formal dialectic, we must dare wish to attain perfection in reality itself, dare think of that extremity of the real which our thought must become.   We no longer need approximate references or advice that is based on past experiences. We only need imagination for those who lack it, courage for those who are afraid.   The only art that still remains to be invented is the art of *making* the revolution; that can begin with a book, a picture, or a film, perhaps also by not hesitating to dream at the top of our voices what everyone is still saying very softly, but this book, this picture, and this film will for the first time be MADE BY ALL, HENCE BY ONE.

This time we must not be afraid of our dream.   Lenin is dead, "Che" is dead. Mao Tse-tung is soon going to die.   Their deaths will not prevent anyone tomorrow from daring to think and do all that they have done, all that they have thought.   Zero is the first figure of a number that never ends.   Let us organize ourselves, beginning with ONE—the Unique without characteristics—in such a way that, advancing more and more quickly and further and further, NOTHING IS EVER ENOUGH FOR ANYONE ANYMORE, NOT EVEN THE OVERTHROW OF AUTHORITY.

Algeria. August 1968.

1. D'HOLBACH, *Le Système social.*
2. Cf. the particularly acute analysis that Henri Lefebvre has just made of the events of May 1968: "L'irruption de Nanterre au sommet," in "L'Homme et la Societé," April-May-June 1968, No. 8.
3. Action committee: "We are on the march."
4. Jean DUBUFFET, *Asphyxiante culture*, J.J. Pauvert, September 1968.
5. This quotation from Lenin, like all the preceding ones, comes from *What's to be done?*, Moscow, Éditions du Progrès, 1966.

The Authors

Jean Cassou, born in 1897, fought in the Spanish Civil War and in the French Resistance during War II. He was among the founders of the Musée National d'Art Moderne, Paris, and served as its chief curator until 1965. At present, he is Director of Studies at the Ecole Pratique des Hautes Etudes, Paris. A novelist, poet, and essayist as well as an art critic, he has published many works in these varied fields.

Michel Ragon, born 1924, resigned his post as Commissioner of the French Pavilion at the 1968 Venice Biennale in protest against the exclusion of foreign artists residing in France and declared his solidarity with the workers' and students' movements. He is an internationally-known novelist, historian, poet, and critic of art and architecture.

André Fermigier, born 1923, served in the administration of schools until 1965. He is art critic of the periodicals *Nouvel Observateur* and *Les Temps Modernes* and has written many books on art.

Gilbert Lascault, born 1934, is First Assistant Professor of Literary Science and Ancient Languages at the University of Nanterre. He contributes to various periodicals such as *Les Temps Modernes*, *Critique*, *L'Arc*, and has published several books on contemporary art.

Gérald Gassiot-Talabot, born 1929, is co-editor of a dictionary of contemporary artists and of a dictionary of modern architecture. He contributes to many periodicals and is a member of the editorial staff of *Opus International*. A student of political science and a member of AICA, he has prepared a number of exhibitions and their catalogs.

Raymonde Moulin holds a doctor's degree in sociology and is a member of the University of Paris and the Centre National de la Recherche Scientifique. She has written numerous articles on the relationship of art and economics and a comprehensive book on the French art market.

Pierre Gaudibert, born 1928, is curator of the Musée d'Art Moderne de la Ville de Paris. He has written essays in the fields of the history and sociology of art on Van Gogh, Poussin, Géricault, and Delacroix as well as books on Ingres and early-nineteenth-century French sculpture.

René Micha, born 1913, is a member of the governing board of Cinématique and of the Film Museum in Brussels. His essays and reviews have been published in various newspapers and periodicals. Two of his films, one about Paul Klee and the other about Paul Delvaux, won prizes in Venice and São Paulo.

Alain Jouffroy, born 1929, is a free-lance writer who lives in Paris. He has written novels, essays, and a number of monographs on such contemporary painters as Victor Brauner, Henri Michaux, and Crippa.